Malaysia

The Business Traveller's Handbook

Gorilla Guides
Travel handbooks for the business jungle

MALAYSIA

First American edition published in 2009 by
INTERLINK TRAVEL
An imprint of Interlink Publishing Group, Inc.
46 Crosby Street
Northampton, Massachusetts 01060
www.interlinkbooks.com

ISBN: 978-1-56656-750-3

Series originator: Max Scott
Series editor: Christopher Ind
Assistant editor: Charles Powell
Design: Nimbus Design
Photography: © Tourism Malaysia
Cartography: Amber Sheers
Printing: Oriental Press, UAE

Every effort has been taken to ensure this Guide is
accurate and up-to-date. The reader is recommended,
however, to verify travel and visa arrangements
before departure. The publishers cannot accept any
responsibility for loss, injury or inconvenience,
however caused.

Malaysia

The Business Traveller's Handbook

Poh Yin Eng

Warm crystalline waters are fringed by white sandy beaches on Redang Island (Pulau Redang).

The skyline of Kuala Lumpur with Merdeka Square in the foreground. This is where the nation celebrates its independence every year on 31 August.

Orang Ulu refers to the numerous tribes that live upriver in Sarawak's vast interior. This tribeswoman is standing next to an elaborately painted mural that decorates her longhouse dwelling. The Orang Ulu are artistic people known for their intricate woodwork, beadwork and tattoos.

With an estimated 4,600 kilometres of coastline, Malaysia is a paradise for beach lovers and water-sports enthusiasts. There are plenty of elegant resorts and luxury lodgings, such as the Shangri-La seen here.

A symbol of the young nation's pride, The Petronas Twin Towers propelled Kuala Lumpur to global city status on its completion in 1998. Although its

Gunung Kinabalu (Mount Kinabalu) stands majestically at 4,095 metres. It is located in the Kinabalu National Park, a World Heritage Site, in the state of Sabah.

reign as the world's tallest building was short lived, it still holds the record for having the highest skybridge.

An Iban boy donning traditional headgear with hornbill feathers. Originally the most feared tribe in Borneo, the Ibans have abandoned their headhunting traditions and have mostly converted to Christianity or Islam.

Acknowledgements

Special thanks to Tourism Malaysia, who kindly supplied the images for this Guide, and to MIDA and MITI for generous access to information and research materials.

A big thank you to my publishers Christopher Ind and Max Scott for giving me the opportunity to write this book. Thanks also to Ming E Wong, without whom this book would never have happened. And to my dearest Vig, who was always there for me and whose support gave me strength until the very end.

Poh Yin Eng
October 2008

Opposite: A vast array of local food is on display at the country's night markets each week. Every suburb will have one or two streets closed to cater to these Pasar Malam (night markets) on different nights of the week.

Contents

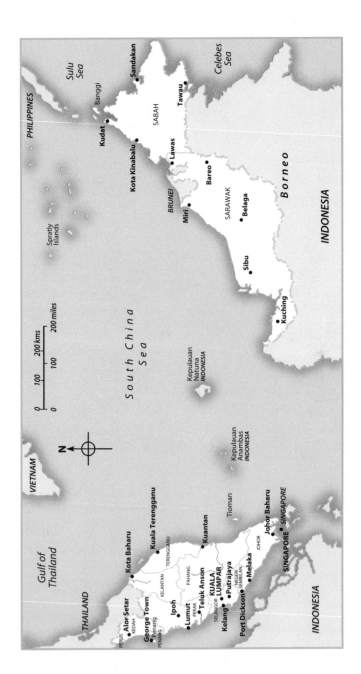

Malaysia

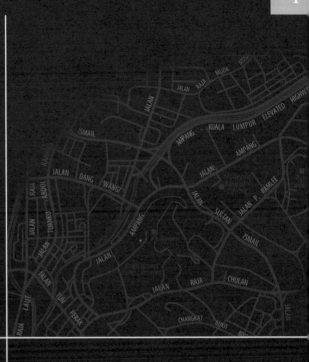

1

Malaysia yesterday and today

Malaysia yesterday and today

A bird's-eye view of the nation,
its history and the special features
that distinguish it from other countries

A condensed history

The modern country

Overview of a nation

Thanks to the ubiquitous marketing campaign by Tourism Malaysia, one can hardly mention Malaysia without hearing the accompanying tagline "Truly Asia". The Tourism Board will have you believe that it deserves its epithet because of Malaysia's unique combination of verdant tropical rainforest which covers more than 70% of the country, the invitingly warm waters off its nearly 4,600km coastline of mostly sandy white beaches and its rich mosaic of cultures due to its multi-ethnic population. Malaysia's neighbours, however, are up in arms, claiming that popular images of Malaysian lifestyle and culture are, in fact, indigenous to other parts of South-East Asia. So, without the credibility to call something their own, what makes Malaysia truly Asia?

To answer this, one needs to look beyond the glossy travel advertisements or brochures and look to its people to find the true pulse of Malaysia. Apart from its immediate neighbour, Singapore, Malaysia is one of the very few truly tolerant multi-racial societies. Nowhere else in the world can you find the dominant ethnic group (Malays, who make up about 50% of the population) living so amicably with such a big and economically powerful minority (ethnic Chinese, about 26%), and together they mix widely with the indigenous tribes (predominantly the Ibans in Sarawak, 11%) and the ethnic Indians (another 7%). In the interest of maintaining peace and harmony, Malaysians took to embracing each other's diversity, creating a warm and friendly society that loves to socialise and celebrate. Visitors are genuinely welcomed into the country and residents find it easy to integrate into a land with a relaxed attitude towards contrast.

Ethnicity

Evidence of the correlation between harmony and contrast is not just found in its people. In Kuala Lumpur, the capital city, towering skyscrapers look down upon wooden houses built on stilts. In sleepy seaside villages, resplendent five-star hotels sit several metres away from centuries-old fishing communities that settled in this part of the world. Geographically, cool hideaways are found in the highlands that roll down to warm, sandy beaches or rich, humid mangroves. Even politically, Malaysia is an Islamic state that has succeeded in balancing religious fundamentalism with pragmatism in application of its laws and business environment.

Development

Having celebrated 50 years of independence in 2007, newly industrialised Malaysia has much to offer the business traveller: well-developed infrastructure and high quality of life available at affordable prices. In its 2008 assessment of 130 economies around the world, the World Economic Forum ranked Malaysia as the 29th most competitive economy in its Index, ahead of many countries in the region. In terms of its readiness to develop technologies in information and communication, Malaysia is also rated among the highest in the region and has ranked number three for Most Attractive Global Offshore Outsourcing Location services in the AT Kearney's 2007 Index.

Geography

Malaysia lies at the crossroads of South-East Asia, halfway between India and China. Its strategic location has made it an essential entrepôt along the maritime spice trade, creating a rich diversity of culture that is centuries old. The country consists of two distinctive areas separated by some 1,000km of the South China Sea. Peninsular Malaysia, also known as West Malaysia, extends southward from the mainland of South-East Asia. To the east of the peninsular, on the northern coast of the island of Borneo, the states of Sabah and Sarawak make up the other part of Malaysia.

Together, it has a total land area of 329,750 square kilometres. Peninsular Malaysia is approximately 132,000km^2, Sabah, 78,000km^2 and Sarawak 120,000km^2. Malaysia is richly endowed with natural resources. It has the world's largest tin deposits and

13 states, 3 federal territories

extensive reserves of oil and gas. Its bountiful forests contain valuable tropical hardwood trees.

The country consists of 13 states and three federal territories of Kuala Lumpur, Putrajaya and Labuan. Politically, the three Wilayah Persekutuan (Federal Territories) formed the 14th state of Malaysia, despite being geographically dispersed. Kuala Lumpur, the nation's capital and largest city, is the seat of parliament, as well as the commercial and financial capital of the country. Putrajaya is the newly created administrative capital for the Federal Government of Malaysia, aimed in part to ease growing congestion within Kuala Lumpur, is situated 25km away.

Peninsula Malaysia

Peninsular Malaysia is about 720km long and 320km wide at its widest point, bounded by Thailand to the north and the South China Sea to the east and separated from the islands of Singapore by the Straits of Johor to the south and from the Indonesian island of Sumatra by the Straits of Malacca to the west.

Location

The Titiwangsa mountain range makes up the central 'spine' of Peninsular Malaysia and the highest peak, Gunung Tahan is 2,183 metres above sea level. The densely forested range starts in the north in Southern Thailand, runs roughly south-east and ends in the south near Jelebu, Negeri Sembilan, Malaysia. The range acts as a natural divider, dividing Peninsular Malaysia into east and west coast regions. Although it makes up only 31% of the country's area, Peninsular Malaysia has more than 80% of its people; most of them are concentrated on the western coast.

Peninsular Malaysia comprises eleven states and two federal territories, Kuala Lumpur and Putrajaya. The most built-up areas are concentrated in state capitals and major cities around the low-lying coastal plains that flank both sides of the Titiwangsa. Apart from a few pockets of mountainous regions which remain untouched, much of the virgin rainforest has been replanted principally with oil palm, although coconut palm and rubber trees are still cultivated for crops in some coastal areas. The recent discovery of offshore oil has propelled tremendous development to the east-coast state of Terengganu.

States of Peninsular Malaysia	State Capital	Population (2007 estimate)
Johor Darul Ta'zim	Johor Barhu	2.74 million
Kedah Darul Aman	Alor Star	1.64 million
Kelantan Darul Naim	Kota Baru	2.1 million
Melaka	Melaka	1 million
Negeri Sembilan Darul Khusus	Seremban	1 million
Pahang Darul Makmur	Kuantan	1.3 million
Perak Darul Ridzuan	Ipoh	2 million
Perlis Indra Kayangan	Kangar	217,500
Pulau Pinang	Georgetown	1.3 million
Selangor Darul Ehsan	Shah Alam	4.19 million
Terengganu Darul Iman	Kuala Terengganu	1.15 million
Federal Territory of Kuala Lumpur		1.8 million
Federal Territory of Putrajaya		30,000

Sabah

Sabah is located at the northern end of the island of Borneo bordering the Sulu Sea, the Celebes Sea and the South China Sea. It is roughly 1,360km east of Peninsular Malaysia and is bounded by Kalimantan (Indonesia) to the south and Sarawak to the west. It has a coastline 1,440km long. A narrow channel separates it from the group of the Philippines. The second largest state of Malaysia, it is known as 'The Land Below the Wind' because of its location being just south of the typhoon-prone region around the Philippines.

Settlement is confined to the coastal fringes since the interior is less accessible because of the mountains. Sabah is home to Mount Kinabalu, the one of the highest mountains in South-East Asia, standing majestically at a height of 4,095m.

Sarawak

This territory is some 640km east of Peninsular Malaysia and has a coastline approximately 720km in length. It is bounded by Kalimantan (Indonesia) to the south and east and by Sabah and Brunei to the north-east. It is the largest state of Malaysia, singly accountable for more than a third of the total land mass.

Sarawak's geographical characteristics are similar to those of the eastern side of Peninsular Malaysia, but in a more extreme form – wider lowlands, longer rivers and yet more dense equatorial forests. The coastal region is low-lying flat country with large extents of swamps and other wet environments that are prone to flooding. Therefore, the hill region provides most of the easily inhabited land and is where most of the larger cities and towns are situated.

States of East Malaysia	State Capital	Population (2007 estimate)
Sabah	Kota Kinabalu	3.4 million
Sarawak	Kuching	2.5 million
Federal Territory of Labuan		76,000

Climate

Malaysia has an equatorial climate, best described as being perennially hot, wet and humid. It lies between one and seven degrees north of the Equator which means temperatures rarely drop below 22°C (72°F), even at night, and typically climbs to 30°C (86°F) or more during the day. The tropics can take some adjusting to, so it may be best to avoid long periods of exposure when you first arrive, especially around midday.

Equatorial climate

Annual rainfall is heavy at 2,500mm (100 inches) and it rains on average 200 days a year. Torrential downpours frequently occur in the late afternoons and evenings, and are often accompany by thunder and lightning. Fortunately, when it does rain, it generally falls in short, strong bursts, except during the height of the monsoon season (November-January). Humidity also tends to hover between 85% and 95%. Because of this, the recommended wardrobe should consist mainly of light and sweat-absorbent material like cotton or linen.

Monsoonal climate

The region has a monsoonal climate, but this affects mainly the east coast of Peninsular Malaysia, as well as some parts of Sabah and Sarawak. This basically means that most coastal activities grind to a halt between October and February in those areas. So, if you are looking to escape to a beach or island resort during this period, head to one on the west coast of the peninsular instead. Even though the east coast is where one can find the most pristine beaches, it is battered by the monsoon winds and currents and, therefore, is too rough and dangerous. The peninsular west coast is wettest between September and December but the coastline remains relatively calm and sheltered. Throughout the region, the dry, and consequently hottest, season is from May to September.

Demography

One of the most interesting aspects of doing business in Malaysia is the multiethnic and multicultural business environment. While race relations continue to be a conversational taboo, the first and most important cultural insight that a successful business traveller needs. Due to centuries of being on the major trading route and the import of labour during the colonial rule, many settlers from around Asia have been long been naturalise and have come to see Malaysia has their homeland. However, as with most migrate groups, these settlers have retained their distinctive culture and religious practices, prevailing even today.

All citizens of Malaysia consider themselves Malaysian first; ethnicity and religion come as a closely related second. The population in 2007 has just exceeded 27 million. Of these, 53% are ethnic Malays, 26% are ethnic Chinese, 8% ethnic Indians and the remaining 13% are formed of many indigenous tribes as well as descedants of mixed European and Asian ancestry, loosely termed Eurasians. There is a small percentage of inter-racial marriages and, although there is a fluid social interaction between the races, families tend to socialise within their own ethnic group – all part of retaining their individual traditions and lifestyles.

The Malays, along with the indigenous people, form a group called Bumiputra, a Bahasa Malaysia term which literally means "sons of the soil". The term accords them special privileges set out in the current constitution and also under the New Economic Policy and you can learn more about them in the History section.

Islam is the official religion of Malaysia and, as required by law, all Malays must be Muslim. Consequently, apostatical Malays must forfeit their Bumiputra status and can no longer consider themselves Malay legally. In spite of this, Muslims in Malaysia generally practise a progressive, tolerant and liberal Islamic doctrine. Muslim women have a more relaxed dress code and those not wearing a *tudung* (a head-scarf that does not cover the face) are not reprimanded or penalised. The country is governed by a secular legal system although there is a Syariah court that is only applicable to Muslims. The Syariah court conducts itself with matters relating to religious and family issues such as marriages, divorces and desertion.

The rest of the population are free to practise their own religion. Most of Chinese in Malaysia are Buddhists who combine Taoist and Confucian practices, while a small number also identify themselves as Christian. The Indians are mostly Hindus but there is also a small minority of Sikhs, Muslims and Christians as well. Christianity has had a greater impact upon East Malaysia, where many indigenous people have converted to Christianity, although others still follow their animist traditions.

Government

Malaysia is a federal parliamentary democracy with a constitutional monarchy. The head of state is Yang di-Pertuan Agong (Supreme Head of State). As the constitutional monarch, he holds office for five years after his election by the conference of Rulers. The role of the Yang di-Pertuan Agong is largely ceremonial as the constitution specifies that executive power is exercised by (or on the advice of) the prime minister and the cabinet. The prime minister is the head of government and federal legislative power is vested in both the government and the bicameral parliament, made up of Dewan Negara (Senate) and Dewan Rakyat (House of Representatives).

History

Malaysia, when compared globally, is a fairly young country. The country was officially formed in 1957 when the Union Jack was lowered for the last time, signalling the end of a long history of colonial rule. The first Malaysian flag was raised in Kuala Lumpur's Merdeka Square at midnight on 31 August 1957. Six years later, the expanded Federation of Malaysia was formed in 1963 through the merging of Malaya and Singapore (which left the Federation soon after) as well as the eastern states of Sabah and Sarawak in Borneo. It was then that the name Malaysia was officially adopted, to reflect the new nation's diverse and racial landscape.

In a short space of time, Malaysia has transformed itself from a fledgling backwater country into one of the fastest growing economies of the world. A look at the history of Malaysia gives a good overview of the dynamics of the region and also what gives rise to the socio-economic factors that exist today.

Ancient history

The oldest known evidence of human habitation is a skull from the Niah Caves in Sarawak dating from 35,000 BC. On the peninsula, Stone Age tools and implements from about 10,000 BC have been found, and some archeologists suggest that they had been left there by the predecessors of the Negrito aborigines, one of the earliest groups to inhabit the peninsula. Present-day examples of these early inhabitants of Malaysia are the Orang Asli (Aboriginal Malays) of the peninsula and indigenous tribes such as the Penan of Sarawak and the Rungus of Sabah, many of whom still pursue a largely nomadic way of life. It is generally believed that Aboriginal Malays began moving down the Malay Peninsula from south-western China about 10,000 years ago.

Independence

At about 2500 BC, anthropologists traced new wave of settlers who migrated to the peninsula from China. Called the Proto-Malays, they were seafarers and farmers, and their advances into the peninsula forced the Negritos into the hills and jungles. Soon after, another group, known as the Deutero-Malays established themselves at around 1000 BC. They were a combination of many peoples – Indians, Chinese, Thai, Arabs, and Proto-Malays – and they had risen by mastering the use of iron. Combined with the peoples of Indonesia, the Deutero-Malays formed the basis for the ethnic group, which today we simply call the Malays.

Early settlers

It is on this basis that the Malays, together with the Orang Asli, identify themselves as the "sons of the soil" (Bumiputra) or the indigenous peoples of Malaysia today. Apart from their common claim to ancient occupation, the various Bumiputra groups also claim to share a common indigenous culture of South-East Asia. This culture is rooted in an agrarian-maritime economy, characterised by a village society led by consensual leadership, whose attitudes were affected by a belief in an omnipresent spiritual world. Although the culture of the Malays in particular came to be highly influenced by Hinduism and then pervaded by Islam, elements of this basic culture can still be found in many Malay cultural practices today.

The early kingdoms

Legend holds that the first Indians were lured to the Malay Peninsula while on an odyssey to uncover the mystical kingdom of Savarnadvipa – the Land of Gold. Blown across the Bay of Bengal by the reliable winds of the southwest monsoon, they arrived in Kedah sometime around 100 BC. Whether or not the civilization they encountered there was the one from the ancient chronicles will probably never be known, but it is certain that the sailors considered the trip lucrative. From that point on, an ever-growing stream of Indian traders arrived in search of gold, aromatic wood and spices. Goods were not the only items exchanged in the peninsula's ports: the Indians also brought a pervasive culture. Hinduism and Buddhism swept through the land, bringing temples and Indian cultural traditions.

The Land of Gold

1

The most tangible illustration of the Hindu-Buddhist period in Malaysian history can be found in Kedah, reputed to be the most ancient state in the country. Archaeological findings at Bujang Valley furnish evidence of a Hindu-Buddhist civilisation that dates back to AD 300. The region was first recorded in Chinese and Sanskrit manuscripts of the seventh and eighth centuries. In subsequent centuries, the area was, however, subjected to the sway of several neighbouring powers, such as the great Sumatra-based civilisation of Sri Vijaya and the Java-based Majapahit empires.

Arrival of Islam and the rise of Malacca

As Muslims conquered India, they began to spread the Islamic religion to Malaysia. The arrival of Islam in this area ended the Hindu-Buddhist period of Malaysian history. Brought primarily by Indian and Arab traders, there is evidence of the presence of the new religion in the region as early as the thirteenth century.

Islam acquired a firm hold on the region when the Hindu ruler of the powerful city state of Malacca, Parameswara Dewa Shah, converted to Islam. According to the Malay Annals, Malacca was founded in 1400 by a prince named Parameswara, who was fleeing from Sumatra. Its rise from a village of royal refugees to a wealthy kingdom was swift. Perfectly located for trade, within 50 years it was the most influential port in South-East Asia. From Malacca, Islam spread to other parts of the Malay states in Sumatra and along the trade routes throughout the Indonesian archipelago.

Once established as the religion of the Malays, Islam profoundly affected Malay society and the Malay way of life. After the collapse of Malacca, the sultanate of Brunei in Kalimantan rose to become the principal agent for the propagation of Islam in that area. The Malay kingdom of Malacca, which dominated both sides of the Straits of Malacca for a hundred years, marked the classical age of Malay culture. Most of the Malay States of the Peninsula today can trace their genesis back to the Malacca sultanate.

1

Colonial Malaysia

With the success and power it enjoyed, Malacca came to control the entire west coast of the Malay Peninsula, the kingdom of Pahang, and much of Sumatra.

At the beginning of the 16th century, the eastern spice trade was routed through Egypt, and no non-Muslim vessel was permitted to dock in Arabian ports. The competing European powers, painfully aware of the need for an open trade route to India and the Far East, sought to establish their own trading ports at the source. In 1511, a Portuguese fleet led by Alfonso de Albuquerque sailed into Malacca's harbour, opened fire with cannon, and captured the city. Malacca's golden age had come to an end, beginning a colonial legacy that would last well into the 20th century.

The Portuguese constructed a massive fort in Malacca – A Famosa, which the Dutch captured in turn in 1641. This would give the Dutch an almost exclusive lock on the spice trade until 1785, when the British East India Company convinced the Sultan of Kedah to allow them to build a fort on the island of Penang. The British were mainly interested in having a safe port for ships on their way to China but, when France captured the Netherlands in 1795, England's reign in the region grew. Rather than hand Malacca over to the French, the Dutch government in exile agreed to let England temporarily oversee the port. The British returned the city to the Dutch in 1808, but it was soon handed back to the British once again in a trade for Bencoolen, Sumatra. The Dutch still largely controlled the region. However, in 1819 Britain sent Sir William Raffles to establish a trading post in Singapore. These three British colonies – Penang, Malacca, and Singapore – came to be known as the Straits Settlements.

The Portuguese

East Malaysia came into British hands via the adventurer Sir James Brooke (who was made Rajah of Sarawak in 1841 after suppressing a revolt against the Sultan of Brunei) and the North Borneo Company (which administered Sabah from 1882). Britain ruled over Malaya until the Japanese invaded and ousted them in 1942.

The Straits Settlements

Independence

The Japanese invasion of Malaya and British Borneo in 1941, which culminated in the humiliating British surrender in Singapore two and a half months later, shattered the region's confidence in their colonial masters and unleashed a new sense of nationalism. During this time, large numbers of Chinese fled to the jungle and established an armed resistance which, after the war's end, would become the basis for an infamous communist insurgency. In 1945, when the Second World War ended, Britain was able to resume interim control. However, faced with mounting resistance, the British were forced to adopt new policies.

The initial formation of the Malayan Union after the war was met with strong opposition. Under the scheme, all the states on the peninsula were to be joined and the status reduced to that of a British colony. Singapore became a separate crown colony and so did both Sarawak and British North Borneo in place of the former Brooke and Chartered Company regimes. In Sarawak, a strong campaign developed opposing the crown colony status and culminated in the assassination of the second British governor (1949).

Consequently, the British were obliged to abandon the Malayan Union scheme, and in 1948 in its place established the Federation of Malaya. The new Federation consisted of all the nine Malay states of the Peninsula, along with Melaka and Pulau Pinang, united under a Federal Government in Kuala Lumpur headed by a British High Commissioner. But this time, the message in the form of a communist insurrection (the Emergency) and the development of a strong Malay nationalist movement (represented by the United Malays National Organisation or UMNO), was clear – Malaysians were ready for independence.

UMNO

United by a common yearning for independence, the main ethnic groups established a political alliance between UMNO and the Malayan Chinese Association (MCA), and were subsequently joined by the Malayan Indian Congress (MIC). When the first federal elections were held in 1955, the newly formed Alliance Party, headed by UMNO, won a near-total victory (51 out of the 52 seats contested), and the UMNO leader, Tunku Abdul Rahman, was appointed the Federation's first Chief Minister.

In the last step towards independence, Tunku Abdul Rahman led a gathering of Malayan rulers and political leaders to London and successfully negotiated the independence of Malaya at the London Conference. He was accorded a hero's welcome on his return and he proclaimed the independence of Malaya on 31 August 1957 in the nation's new capital Kuala Lumpur.

Recent history

The formation of present-day Federation of Malaysia began in 1961 after the Tunku convinced Singapore, Sabah and Sarawak to join Malaya in a federal union. The formation of Malaysia was opposed by both the Philippines and Indonesia, as each had territorial claims on East Malaysia.

Non-violent opposition came from the Philippines, which claimed ownership of Sabah until early in 1978. The hostility of Indonesia was, however, more vehement. Indonesia's president, Sukarno, described the federation as a British imperialist subterfuge and waged an undeclared war against Malaysia (Konfrontasi). As the conflict escalated in the jungles of Borneo, Malaysia received military aid from Great Britain and other Commonwealth nations. In 1963, a meeting was held in Manila to resolve the cross-border issues. Based on the findings of a United Nations mission, the Sabah and the people of Sabah and Sarawak were in favour of Malaysia. Malaysia was officially recognised by the UN on 16 September 1963. Nevertheless, hostilities continued until President Sukarno's fall from power in Indonesia (1965) and have, to this day, never officially been declared to be over.

Meanwhile, on the other side of the peninsula, the merger with Singapore was proceeding far from satisfactorily. Friction had developed between Malay leaders and Singapore's prime minister, Lee Kuan Yew. Politics in Malaysia at this time were mainly Malay-based, with an emphasis on special privileges for the

MIC

Tunku Abdul Rahman

Malays, a provision that has existed since British colonial rule. Singapore's People's Action Party (PAP) and Malaysia's Democratic Action Party (DAP) both sought to equalise the position of the Chinese minority within the Malaysian Federation. Heated arguments with the ruling UMNO party about the nature of Malay privileges, with the mostly Chinese opposition mounting a "Malaysian Malaysia" campaign had contributed to the separation of Singapore on 9 August 1965.

The worst was yet to come. Events leading to the Malaysia-Singapore separation had started to inflame the fragile racial relations. The Chinese and Indians resented Malay-backed plans favouring the majority, including one to make Malay the official school and government language. The Malays, in turn, felt slighted by their comparable economic disadvantage. In 1969, after the opposition party, DAP, won a significant number of seats in the general elections, riots swept through Kuala Lumpur. Etched deeply into Malaysia's modern history as the "May 13th Incident", the unrest lasted two months, led to a 22-month suspension of parliament and placed the young nation in a state of emergency which, in truth, has not been lifted to this day.

May 13th Incident

When parliamentary rule was reinstated in 1971, Barisan Nasional (National Front), successor to the Alliance Party, took office. Still headed by 'Malay-centric' UMNO leaders, the new government sought to placate the Malay community and achieve greater economic balance with the Malaysian New Economic Policy (NEP). Implemented despite the international and internal opposition, the NEP is essentially an affirmative action programme for every Bumiputra. Literally translated, it means "earth son" or "son of the soil" and embraces ethnic Malays, Javanese, Bugis, Minang and occasionally other indigenous ethnic groups such as the Orang Asli in Peninsular Malaysia and the indigenous tribes in Sabah and Sarawak. Examples of NEP policies include quotas for the following: admission to government educational institutions, qualification for public scholarships, positions in government and ownership in business. Today, Bumiputras make up about 65% of the population.

NEP

The success of the policies is a subject of a much-heated debate. But in the subsequent years, Malaysia has undergone tremendous growth and prosperity, and has arguably made significant progress in race relations. Many attribute the country's success to the dynamic leadership of Prime Minister Dato' Sri Mahathir bin Mohamad, who led the country from 1981 until 2003.

As the fourth Malaysian prime minister, Mahathir Mohamad instituted economic reforms that would transform Malaysia into one of the five "Asian Tigers". He launched an aggressive campaign to turn Malaysia's economy from being primarily agricultural-based to one concentrated towards manufacturing and electronics. His legacy permeates modern Malaysia – the soaring steel and glass towers of Petronas Towers, the first national car, the third longest suspension bridge in the world, the most modern and high tech airport, and a host of other high profile megaprojects, propelled, no doubt, by the double digit GDP growth rates throughout the early and mid nineties.

Beginning in 1997 and continuing through the next year, Malaysia suffered from the Asian currency crisis. Instead of following the economic prescriptions of the International Monetary Fund and the World Bank, the prime minister opted for fixed exchange rates and capital controls. In late 1999, Malaysia was on the road to economic recovery, and it appeared Mahathir's measures were working.

Asian currency crisis

Yet in the midst of economic uncertainty, Mahathir sacked his heir apparent, Anwar Ibrahim, from his posts as deputy prime minister and finance minister in September 1998, after a disagreement over how to deal with the country's economic problems. In defiance, Anwar launched a reform movement attacking the government. The prime minister then jailed Anwar, who was beaten and convicted on trumped-up charges of corruption and sodomy. Harsh criticisms poured in internationally and also from within Anwar's strong supporters in Malaysia. In 2004, a year after Mahathir left office, Malaysia's high court overturned Anwar's conviction, releasing the former deputy prime minister, who had served six years in prison.

1

Abdullah Badawi

In October 2003, Mahathir retired after 22 years in office. His rule led to his country's enormous economic growth but was also characterised by repression and human rights abuses. Malaysia's new prime minister, Abdullah Badawi, has a less draconian reputation, earning him the affectionate nickname – Pak Lah (Malay diminutive for "Uncle Abdullah"). In his first year in office he made headway on reducing corruption and instituting reforms by making several high-profile arrests for corruption. In March 2004, the ruling Barisan Nasional (National Front) coalition won an astonishing 90% of parliamentary seats, and Abdullah Badawi was reflected on his own merits.

2008 elections

However, in March 2008's parliamentary elections, Barisan Nasional under Prime Minister Badawi and his leading party, UMNO, suffered a major setback for the first time since Malaysia's independence. Opposition parties quadrupled their representation in Parliament, and Badawi's coalition, although it won 140 of 222 seats in parliament; lost its two-thirds majority, necessary to amend the constitution. In addition, the opposition also won 5 of 13 state legislatures, as opposed to only one in the last election.

The aftermath of the March elections has led to a regime crisis within UMNO, with the majority of its members, including former prime minister Dr Mahathir Mohammad, calling on Abdullah Badawi to take full responsibility on the dismal performance and step down as party leader. The dispute culminated in the resignation of Dr Mahathir from UMNO in May 2008, after serving 22 years as the party's president. He announced that he was quitting the party after having lost confidence in Abdullah Badawi's leadership and that he would only rejoin the party after Badawi had stepped down as UMNO president and prime minister. Amid mounting pressure, Badawi announced he would step down as UMNO president and prime minister in June 2010

The true economic implications of Malaysia's first major political shake-up remains to be seen. Yet in the months following the elections, the general consensus is that the political climate has come of age, evident in the move away from communal politics fostered by UMNO for the past half-century to divide voters along ethnic lines. The strong wins by the opposition parties not only signalled a yearning for change, but also for greater equality; evident in the cross-ethnic voting with Malays voting for the ethnic Chinese-based Democratic Action Party (DAP) and the non-Malays readily backing the Islamist Parti Islam Se-Malaysia (PAS). Among the first steps taken by opposition-controlled state governments was a move to renounce the New Economic Policy, which discriminates against Chinese and Indians in education, business and government jobs.

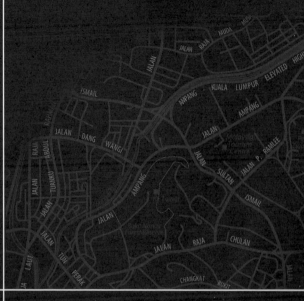

2

investigating the potential market

investigating the potential market

An outline of some of the myriad organisations which exist to assist the exporter, along with an assessment of their focus and likely relevance

Before arrival

The business traveller, should, of course, be as well informed as possible before entering a new market. This chapter acts as a guide to where to find this information. It includes government and private sources in electronic and hard copy format and discusses the availability of reliable market and economic information.

Whether you are visiting Malaysia for the first time or making the latest in a series of regular visits, preparation is essential to get the most out of the trip and ensure that your project succeeds. Obtaining the latest information will allow you to plan effectively for your visit, get a clear picture of the market you are entering, identify any trends or opportunities that you can use to your advantage and spot any pitfall. It is equally important to ensure that the information you use is accurate and that you are aware of any bias.

After decades of aggressive economic reforms and pro-business policies, Malaysia is now one of the most pleasant, hassle-free countries in South-East Asia to visit and do business in. The Malaysian government heavily promotes foreign investments by offering attractive tax and other incentives for investors. Combined with key factors such as the quality and affordability of the infrastructure, political stability and cultural adaptability of the skilled workforce – the result: a buoyant and vibrant business environment.

Business friendly

The accessibility of this country is also reflected in the easy access to a wide range of relevant business and trade information. The sources below can provide a starting point for research on the Malaysia market and many of them are free or provide information at very little cost.

Malaysian Embassies and High Commissions

Malaysia has 104 missions worldwide and also has 52 Honorary Consuls General / Consuls abroad.

Australia
The High Commission of Malaysia
7, Perth Avenue Yarralumla, ACT 2600

2

The Commonwealth of Australia
Tel: +61 2 6273 154-3/5/6
Fax: +61 2 6273 4340/ 2496
Website: www.malaysia.org.au
Email: malcanberra@netspeed.com.au

China
Embassy of Malaysia
No. 2, Liang Ma Qiao Bei Jie,
Chaoyang District, 100600 Beijing,
People's Republic of China
Tel: +86 10 6532 253-1/2/3
Fax: +86 10 6532 5032
Email: mwbjing@kln.gov.my

Germany
Embassy of Malaysia
Klingelhoeferstr. 6, 10785 Berlin
Federal Republic of Germany
Tel: +49 30 88 57 49 0
Fax: +49 30-88 57 49 50/55
Email: mwberlin@malemb.de

India
High Commission of Malaysia,
50-M, Satya Marg, Chanakyapuri,
110 021 New Delhi
Republic of India
Tel: +91 11 2611 129-1/2/3/7
Fax: +91 11 2688 1538
Email: maldelhi@kln.gov.my

Japan
Embassy of Malaysia
20-16, Nanpeidai-Cho, Shibuya-Ku,
Tokyo 150-0036
Japan
Tel: +81 3 3476 3840
Fax: +81 3 3476 4971
Email: maltokyo@kln.gov.my

United Kingdom
Malaysian High Commission
45-46 Belgrave Square
London SW1X 8QT

United Kingdom of Great Britain and Northern Ireland
Tel: +44 20 7235 8033
Fax: +44 20 7235 5161
Email: mwlon@btconnect.com

USA
Embassy of Malaysia
3516 International Court, N.W.
Washington, DC 20008
United States of America
Tel: +1 202 572 9700
Fax: +1 202 572 9882
Email: malwashdc@kln.gov.my

For contact details of the Malaysian embassy or
consular office nearest to you, access the informative
website of Malaysia's Ministry of Foreign Affairs at
www.kln.gov.my. It can also tell you whether your
country has a foreign mission appointed by Malaysia.

Ministries, Government Agencies and Business Organisations

A natural first port of call would be the ministry or
agency in your country that is responsible for the
development of trade and industry. The following
countries' websites provide invaluable information
relevant to helping you gain an understanding of the
business environment in Malaysia. So even though these
sites may provide information with slant towards their
respective countries' businesses, the learning they provide
is generally applicable and therefore worth exploring.

UK

The primary British government source for information
on overseas markets is the **UK Trade & Investment**
(UKTI), which brings the export development and
promotion resources of the Department of Trade and
Industry and the Foreign and Commonwealth Office into
one organisation. British companies looking to start up
or expand their overseas business interests will find that
UKTI can advise them on their business sector, help them
to assess risks and inform them about investment
promotion and protection agreements. It also offers
two chargeable services: Overseas Market Introduction

UKTI

Service (OMIS) and the Export Marketing Research Scheme (EMRS) that can target local contacts and find information tailor-made for you.

For enquiries:
UK Trade & Investment
Kingsgate House
66-74 Victoria Street
London SW1E 6SW
Tel: +44 (0)20 7215 8000
Mobile: +44 (0)7825 603103
Website: www.uktradeinvest.gov.uk

US

The **US State Department** provides a wide range of information to US companies or representatives of US companies operating in Malaysia. The Country Commercial Guide and other industry-specific market research can be obtained by registering or for a small fee: www.state.gov/travelandbusiness/

American businesses can contact the **US Department of Commerce**, the world's largest business federation representing more than 3 million businesses of all sizes, sectors, and regions. It includes hundreds of associations, thousands of local chambers, and more than 100 American Chambers of Commerce in 91 countries. Members range from large Fortune 500 companies to home-based, one-person operations. In fact, 96% of membership encompasses businesses with fewer than 100 employees. The Chamber tracks the development and effects of US trade agreements with other nations and champions free trade with US government agencies and authorities: www.uschamber.com

The **US Department of Commerce International Trade Commission** is another helpful source of information. To find out about trade events across the United States and the world that focus on exporting, international business and other industry topics: www.export.gov

The **US-ASEAN Business Council** was originally an initiative of the US State Department. Today, it is an independent grouping of established companies such as General Electric and Abbott Laboratories which have

2

banded together to promote and protect American business interests in the ASEAN region which Malaysia is an integral part of. The Council provides up-to-date business and political news as well as country reports and welcomes business enquiries. With over two decades of strategic alliances and relationships building, the Council has helped improve the business environment for American companies and expand the US competitive position in the region.

US-ASEAN Business Council
1101 17th Street, NW
Suite 411
Washington, DC 20036
United States of America
Tel: +1 202 289 1911
Fax: +1 202 289 0519
Email: mail@ usasean.org
Website: www.us-asean.org

Australia

The Australian Trade Commission or Austrade is the federal government's export and investment facilitation agency. The Austrade website provides advice to Australian companies on general export issues, assistance in determining which overseas markets hold potential for their products, and aid in building a presence in the market. Through their network of global offices, Austrade can assist with finding potential business partners or agents, prepare publicity material, organise product launches and offer assistance with attending suitable trade exhibitions. Australian companies can also take up a free listing within the website, thus being included into a searchable database of products and services.

Under their Export Market Development Grant (EMDG) scheme, Austrade provides eligible Australian companies with financial support via a reimbursement scheme. The grant covers part of the costs incurred on eligible export promotion activities to encourage small and medium sized Australian businesses to develop export markets. www.austrade.gov.au

EMDG

2

Malaysian ministries and government agencies

Malaysia has evolved from being predominantly a tin and rubber exporter into a modern industrialised nation. This is due, in no small part, to the efforts of a pro-business government and specially created trade and industry promotion agencies. The purpose of these agencies is to attract foreign investments to promote international trade. These sites are packed full with information and give excellent (albeit with much hard sell) local market background.

Ministry of International Trade and Industry (MITI)

The Ministry's primary role is to encourage foreign and domestic investment by formulating and implementing policies on industrial development and investment. It is also the regulating body for most matters involving foreign businesses, ownership and trade. The MITI website gives a clear overview of the various government agencies and their functions in assisting business organisations of all scales. Investors and entrepreneurs can download application forms to ease their incentive application process. However, to make sense of which forms to fill, it is best to refer to the specific agency that is supported by MITI (see below). Another way to work through the maze is to sign up. Registration is free and once registered, you can access specific industries or find business partners, receive relevant advice and updates.

MITI

Ministry of International Trade and Industry
Block 10, Government Offices Complex, Jalan Duta
50622 KL, Kuala Lumpur, Malaysia
Tel: +60 3 6203 3022
Fax: +60 3 6201 2337
Email: webmiti@miti.gov.my
Website: www.miti.gov.my

Malaysian Industrial Development Authority (MIDA)

The most relevant, and easily, most rewarding source of information base for foreign companies can be found on the MIDA website. The Malaysian Industrial Development Authority (MIDA) is the government's principal agency for the promotion and coordination of foreign industrial development and investment into

MIDA

2

Malaysia. Companies looking to invest in Malaysia can learn about how to benefit from investment incentives such as corporate tax holidays, government grants of land, duty-free imports and joint-venture opportunities.

Other facilities include comprehensive guide for investors, a searchable database of companies under 'Matchmaking Enterprise' and excellent online library of informative MIDA publications that are available for free download. Long-term business strategists will find publications such as "Cost of Doing Business", "Expatriate Living", and various guides to key sectors in Malaysia to be a great introduction to the government's support and policies for foreign businesses. There are also many overseas representative offices in key cities in the US, Europe and Asia Pacific. For a complete listing, see their website.

Malaysian Industrial Development Authority (MIDA)
Block 4, Plaza Sentral
Jalan Stesen Sentral 5
Kuala Lumpur Sentral
50470 Kuala Lumpur
Malaysia
Tel: +60 3 2267 3633
Fax: +60 3 2274 7970
Email: promotion@mida.gov.my
Website: www.mida.gov.my

Malaysian External Trade Development Corporation (MATRADE)

MATRADE, Malaysia External Trade Development Corporation, is Malaysia's national trade promotion agency. Assisted by a network of 34 overseas offices located in major commercial cities around the world, MATRADE provides a wide range of services and assistance to both Malaysian exporters and foreign importers who are sourcing for trade-related information. The website features a searchable database which comprises manufacturers, contract manufacturers, trading companies, service providers and trade associations.

MATRADE

2

Malaysia External Trade Development Corporation
Menara MATRADE
Jalan Khidmat Usaha
Off Jalan Duta
50480 Kuala Lumpur
Malaysia
Tel: +60 3 6207 7077
Fax: 3 6203 7037 / 7033
Email: info@matrade.gov.my
Website: www.matrade.gov.my

MSC Malaysia (Formerly Multimedia Super Corridor)
Another economic restructuring legacy of former Prime
Minister Tun Dr Mahathir Mohammad, MSC Malaysia
refers to the government initiative to create Malaysia's
'Silicon Valley'. Incentives such as land, tax breaks,
special education programmes to ensure workforce
supply for the global information and communication
technology (ICT) industry makes it worthwhile, especially
for ICT-related companies, to acquaint themselves with
the information available on the website.

Multimedia Development Corporation (MDeC)
MSC Malaysia Headquarters
Persiaran APEC
63000 Cyberjaya
Selangor, Malaysia
Tel: 1800 888 338 (Toll free, within Malaysia only)
Tel: +60 3 8315 3000
Fax: +60 3 8315 3115
E-mail: clic@mdec.com.my
Website: www.msc.com.my

Suruhanjaya Syarikat Malaysia
Suruhanjaya Syarikat Malaysia (Companies Commission
of Malaysia) or SSM is a statutory body regulating

SSM   companies and businesses. All companies wishing to
operate in Malaysia must register at SSM (Companies
Division). Under the regulations of the Companies
Commission of Malaysia, there are different procedures
for local companies and foreign companies. There are
offices in every state in Malaysia. For more local listings,
check the website which is in both Bahasa Malay and
English.

Syarikat Malaysia
Head Office (Kuala Lumpur)
Tingkat 2 & 10-19, Putra Place
100 Jalan Putra
50622 Kuala Lumpur
Tel: +60 3 4047 6000
Fax: +60 3 4047 6317
Hotline: +60 3 4047 6111 / 6222
E-mail: enquiry@ssm.com.my
Website: www.ssm.com.my

Further sources of information

This is not a definitive list of bodies and merely indicates
the types of organisations that exist and how they may
help. Most of the website links provided are not only
informative but can act as a springboard to further links
that support businesses or specific industries.

Chambers of Commerce and Trade Associations

Some of these are especially relevant for business
travellers as they are the bilateral business
representations of your home country and Malaysia.
Because of Malaysia's established trading history, there
are many such organisations. Some of the more active
organisations are listed below. Most of the websites
provide information on conferences, events, trade fairs,
shows and exhibitions that are excellent opportunities
for networking, information gathering or just meeting
up with your countrymen to exchange experiences.
The full list can be found in Appendix 1.

American Malaysian Chamber of Commerce (AmCham)
11.03 – 11.05 Level 11
AMODA Building
22 Jalan Imbi
55100 Kuala Lumpur
Malaysia
Tel: +60 3 2148 2407
Fax: +60 3 2142 8540
Email: info@amcham.com.my
Website: www.amcham.com.my

2

Malaysia Australia Business Council (MABC)
Quest Business Center
3rd Floor, Wisma RKT No 2
Jalan Raja Abdullah,
50300 Kuala Lumpur
Malaysia
Tel: +60 3 2695 3121
Fax: +60 3 2695 3128
Email: mabc@mabc.org.my
Website: www.mabc.org.my

British Malaysian Chamber of Commerce (BMCC)
LOT E05A1, 5th Floor, East Block
Wisma Selangor Dredging
142B Jalan Ampang,
50450 Kuala Lumpur.
Malaysia
Tel: +60 3 2163 1784
Fax: +60 3 2163 1781
Website: www.bmcc.org.my

NCCIM

The National Chamber of Commerce and Industry
of Malaysia (NCCIM) is an umbrella organisation
bringing together five principal Malaysian private
sector organisations concerned with trade and industry.
Additional local trade support can also be found on two
of the more notable websites that are linked to NCCIM
(the rest can be found in Appendix 1).

**The National Chamber of Commerce and Industry
of Malaysia (NCCIM)**
6A, 6th Floor, Menara BGI
Plaza Berjaya
12 Jalan Imbi
55100 Kuala Lumpur
Malaysia
Tel: 03-2141 9600
Fax: 03-2141 3775
Email: enquiry@nccim.org.my
Website: www.nccim.org.my

**Malaysian International Chamber of Commerce and
Industry (MICCI)**
Headquarters
C-8-8, Block C

Plaza Mont' Kiara
2 Jalan Kiara
Mont' Kiara
50480 Kuala Lumpur
Malaysia
Tel: +60 3 6201 7708
Fax: +60 3 6201 7705 / 06
E-mail: micci@micci.com
Website: www.micci.com

Federation of Malaysian Manufacturers (FMM)
No 3 Persiaran Dagang
PJU 9, Bandar Sri Damansara
52200 Kuala Lumpur
Tel: +60 3 6276 1211
Fax: +60 3 6274 1266
Email: webmaster@fmm.org.my
Website: www.fmm.org.my

FFM

Useful websites and resources

Malaysia, like the rest of Asia Pacific, has a largely
internet-savvy population. While the government and
businesses have only just begun catching up with the
population's love for e-literacy, you can doubtlessly find
a link to provide, if not the answer, then at the very least,
an idea of where to look for a business-related query.
Here are just some to get you started:

Government, business and trade
Malaysian Government Online – www.gov.my
Kuala Lumpur Regional Centre for Arbitration –
www.rcakl.org.my
Securities Commission of Malaysia – www.sc.com.my
Kuala Lumpur Stock Exchange – www.klse.com.my
Credit Guarantee Corporation –
www.iguarantee.com.my
Export-Import Bank of Malaysia Berhad –
www.exim.com.my
Franchise Association – www.mfa.org.my
Ministry of Agriculture – www.agrolink.moa.my
Royal Customs and Excise Dept of Malaysia –
www.customs.gov.my
Immigration Department – www.imi.gov.my
Department of Environment – www.doe.gov.my

Special Taskforce to Facilitate Business or PEMUDAH –
www.pemudah.gov.my
National Productivity Corporation (NPC) –
www.npc.org.my
Business Licensing Electronic Support System –
www.bless.gov.my

General
All Malaysia – www.allmalaysia.info
Malaysia Expat – www.malaysia.alloexpat.com

News and media
Malaysian National News Agency – www.bernama.com
The Edge Daily – www.theedgedaily.com
The Star – www.thestar.com.my
New Straits Times Press – www.nst.com.my
NSTP e-media group of publications – www.nstp.com.my

Travel and tourism
Tourism Malaysia – www.tourism.gov.my
Virtual Malaysia – www.virtualmalaysia.com
Asia Travel Guide – www.asiatravel.com/malaysia.html
Asia Tour Guide –
www.asiatour.com/malaysia/content1.htm

Economic and country guides
Once you have gained an overview of the market in
Malaysia, you may want more detailed economic
information or wish to concentrate on your particular
sector. This is where the cost of research starts to
increase. Armed with detailed information, the risk of
unpleasant surprises later on will be much reduced. You
will also be aware of the trends and the possible effects
on your business and therefore able to plan for them.

Dun and Bradstreet (D&B)
D&B is the leading source of business information and
insight, enabling companies to implement sound business
strategies. They produce Country Report and Country
Risk Report on Malaysia that is updated regularly and
available only on subscription. These reports can be
found under their 'Risk Management' products and is
designed to help you evaluate risks associated with cross-
border transactions. Within these reports, you can find

information, in varying degrees of depth, on payment terms, economic forecasts and latest developments of the country.

On their general corporate website, you can also request business reports and credit rating on any company in their extensive and up-to-date international business database. D&B can also support marketing and sales efforts with their selection of directories and marketing database.

For information relating to D&B's Country Risk Services, see http://www.dnbcountryrisk.com/

UK and International Enquiry
Tel: +44 1628 492700
Fax: +44 1628 492929
E-mail: CountryRisk@dnb.com

USA
Tel: 1 800 234 3867 ext 7002
E-mail: CountryRiskServices@dnb.com

For general enquires about D&B's full range of products and business solution tools, log onto www.dnb.com or www.dnb.co.uk

Economist Intelligence Unit

EIU

The Economist Intelligence Unit is another source of independent economic and political forecast. Its flagship product is the Country Report analysing the latest economic and political developments, reviewing changes in local government policies and providing information on key data and statistics on output, prices, inflation, exchange rates, loans, retail sales, imports and exports and foreign direct investment. Country Reports can be purchased as an annual subscription, a single issue or on a per article basis. Monthly reports for the largest countries are only available if you choose to access your reports online. Print customers will receive a quarterly aggregated report for those countries.

EIU
26 Red Lion Square

London WC1R 4HQ
United Kingdom
Tel: +44 (0)20 7576 8181
Fax: +44 (0)20 7576 8476
E-mail: london@eiu.com
Website: www.eiu.com

or

The Economist Building
111 West 57th Street
New York NY 10019
United States of America
Tel: +1 (212) 554 0600
Fax: +1 (212) 586 1181/2
E-mail: newyork@eiu.com

Oxford Business Group

The Oxford Business Group also publishes annually an
economic and political intelligence report on Malaysia.
The report examines developments in politics, economy
and as well as key sectors such as banking, capital
markets, energy, infrastructure, industry and insurance.

Annual Business Economic and Political Review:
Malaysia can be purchased online in full (print or soft
copy) or in downloadable chapters (soft copy only).

Oxford Business Group
33 St James's Square
London SW1Y 4JS
United Kingdom
Tel: +44 (0)20 7403 7213
Email: sales@oxfordbusinessgroup.com
Website: www.oxfordbusinessgroup.com

3

getting to Malaysia

getting to Malaysia

The various considerations
in arranging travel to Malaysia

Visa requirements

Most travellers from Europe, the United Kingdom, the United States, Australia and commonwealth countries (except India, Pakistan, Bangladesh, Sri Lanka, Nigeria) will find it easy to enter Malaysia since no visa is required for short stays. However, since immigration and travel regulations are subject to change, it is best to check ahead even if you are from a visa-exempt country.

3

Visitors from visa-exempt countries will be issued a social visit pass at immigration checkpoints upon presentation of a passport or internationally recognised travel document that must be valid for more than six months from the date of entry into Malaysia, together with a completed Arrival/Departure Card (available at checkpoints and on major airlines). The social visit pass is issued free of charge and is valid for a business traveller visiting Malaysia for social, business or academic purposes (except for employment). Do a thorough check with your counterparts and also on the immigration website to ascertain if your purpose of visit fall into the correct category.

The duration of stay allowed under the social visit differs between the different nationalities and usually ranges from 14 days to 3 months. Before leaving the checkpoint, check carefully that the pass has been stamped clearly onto your passport and take note of the social visit pass duration given to you. Over-staying is a punishable offence in Malaysia and you may also be detained during departure if a valid stamp cannot be found in your passport (more common with checkpoint entry by land).

A visitor may be required, in some instances, to present proof of his or her financial ability to finance his/her stay in Malaysia together with a confirmed departure ticket. Please note that a valid passport (and visa, if applicable) is also required for travel between Peninsular Malaysia and the East Malaysian states of Sabah and Sarawak, and when travelling between Sabah and Sarawak.

Foreign nationals who require a visa to enter Malaysia must apply and obtain a visa in advance at a Malaysian Representative Office before entering the country.

3

Nationals of these countries require visas for any purpose of visiting Malaysia:

> Afghanistan, Angola, Bangladesh, Bhutan, Burkina Faso, Burundi, Cameroon, Central African Republic, China, Colombia, Comoros, Congo Democratic Republic, Congo Republic, Cote D'Ivoire, Equatorial Guinea, Eritrea, Ethiopia, Ghana, Guinea – Bissau, Hong Kong (Certificate of Identity), India, Liberia, Mali, Mozambique, Myanmar (normal passport), Nepal, Nigeria, Pakistan, Rwanda, Sri Lanka, Serbia & Montenegro, Taiwan, United Nations (Laissez Passer), and Western Sahara

Nationals of these countries require special approval from the Ministry of Home Affairs to enter Malaysia:

> Israel, Serbia, Montenegro

MoFA

Visitors should be aware that possessing and dealing in drugs carries the death penalty in Malaysia. Full details of visa requirements for different nationals are provided on the Immigration Department of Malaysia's website at www.imi.gov.my or Ministry of Foreign Affairs Malaysia website at www.kln.gov.my

Work permits

The work permit is the most important form of documentation required for expatriates seeking employment in the country. Normally, this is obtained by the employer for the employee, upon arrival in the country. The work permit application process is bureaucratic and can be lengthy. Employers will often deal with the paperwork on behalf of their expatriate employees but some companies and individuals opt to use the services of an agency. Permits are given for varying periods from six months to several years. Dependants of employment pass holders are not allowed to work unless they obtain a permit in their own right.

There are several work permits or passes available, depending on the nature of your employment in Malaysia. They are:

1. **Visit Pass (Temporary Employment)** This is issued to persons who enter the country to take up employment for less than 24 months or earn a monthly income of less than RM3,000.
2. **Employment Pass** This is issued to foreigners who enter the country to take up employment for a minimum period of two years and earn a monthly income of more than RM2,500.
3. **Visit Pass (Professional)** This is issued to foreigners who wish to enter the country for the purpose of engaging on short-term contract in these professions:
   - artists
   - filmmakers
   - researchers recognised by the Government of Malaysia
   - members of an International Organisation
   - volunteers
   - invited lecturers/speakers
   - those entering for religious purposes
   - experts in the installation or maintenance of machines/computers
   - trainees or technical trainees (e.g. management trainees in hotels and resorts)

There are restrictions on the number of expatriate workers that can be employed by companies, depending on the company's level of foreign paid-up capital. For executive posts requiring professional qualifications and practical experience, expatriates may be employed up to a maximum period of ten years, subject to the condition that Malaysians are trained to eventually take over the posts. For non-executive posts requiring technical skills and experience, expatriates may be employed up to a maximum period of five years while Malaysians are trained to take over the posts. It is not known to what extent these conditions are enforced.

An expatriate executive transferred from one post to another post within the same company is not required to obtain a new employment pass. A new expatriate executive whether replacing or filling a new expatriate post, is required to obtain a new employment pass. All holders of employment passes are issued with multiple entry visas valid for the corresponding period that the

3

employment pass is valid. Malaysia practises stringent laws prohibiting foreigners from working in the country without authorisation and frequently detains or deports illegal workers. Visitors and expatriates should therefore strictly follow immigration laws and regulations.

For further information on the employment of expatriates, you can download a PDF copy of 'Guidebook on the Employment of Expatriates' on the Malaysian Industrial Development Authority (MIDA) website: www.mida.gov.my

Malaysia as a second home

To encourage people to retire in Malaysia or spend several months a year here, the Malaysian government has recently introduced "Malaysia My Second Home" Programme (MM2H). It replaces the previous 'Silver Hair' programme. The MM2H programme is available to most foreign nationals of all ages. Under the scheme, the main applicant is allowed to bring their dependants and one domestic helper to live in Malaysia. Successful applicants are given a five-year renewable visa (but not permanent residence status) and other privileges. Overseas personal income is tax-exempt and applicants can bring all their household effects and may import one car duty-free into Malaysia, or may acquire a car in Malaysia free of duty.

To qualify for the scheme, applicants aged above 50 years must meet one of the following conditions, while those who are below 50 must meet both:

1. A fixed deposit account (in a local Malaysian bank) of RM150,000 if married or RM100,000 if single. The funds have to be left in the bank during the period of validity of the visa.

2. A fixed monthly income over RM10,000 if married or RM7,000 if single. This could be a pension, dividends or other forms of regular income. Documentary evidence is required as proof of income.

A sponsor in Malaysia may also be required, but this condition is sometimes relaxed. Employment in Malaysia

3

is prohibited under this scheme unless specific approval is obtained. To find out more, visit the website: www.mm2h.gov.my

Permanent residence and citizenship

If you wish to apply to be a permanent resident of Malaysia you must have lived in the country continuously for at least five years under a valid Entry Permit, or at least ten years in the case of foreign husbands of Malaysian citizens.

A foreigner over the age of 21 can apply to the National Registration Department to become a citizen of Malaysia by naturalisation if they have been a permanent resident for at least 12 years and lived in Malaysia for not less than ten of these years, including the 12 months immediately prior to application. They must also be able to prove an adequate knowledge of the Malay language. The Malaysian government does not recognize dual citizenship so applicants granted citizenship are required to relinquish the citizenship of any other country.

Travelling to Malaysia

Flights

Most international visitors will arrive in Malaysia's main international airport – Kuala Lumpur International Airport. Commonly known as KLIA, it is located in Sepang, 50 kilometres from Kuala Lumpur city centre. The gleaming airport was built in 1998, in time for the 1998 Commonwealth Games, and is another megaproject first conceived by then Prime Minister Dr. Mahathir Mohammed. It occupies a site of 100 square kilometres and is considered one of the largest airport sites in the world. The airport is served by 57 international airlines and is currently ranked as the 13th busiest airport in the world by international passenger traffic in 2007. KLIA has won numerous awards from international organisations such as Skytrax and International Air Transport Association as one of the top airports in the world. Malaysia Airlines, the country's national carrier, has also won numerous international awards for its standards of service. It operates flights worldwide as well as on domestic routes from KLIA.

Flights

KLIA

3

The main airport building is split into two terminals, domestic and international, well connected by Aerotrains that come at three to five minute intervals. The passenger complex is bright and airy, thanks to the huge expanse of glass throughout the building and the glass air-wells for natural light to filter in. Within these covered air-wells, transplanted trees from secondary rainforest thrive, surrounding the airport with green spaces. The airport terminals have complimentary Wi-Fi facilities, as well as a comprehensive range of retail and food outlets to occupy those with time to spare.

LCCT

There is also a Low Cost Carrier Terminal (LCCT) extension located 15 minutes bus ride away from the main KLIA terminals. The bus ride cost RM1.50 and comes at a 30-minute interval. The LCCT was specifically built at KL International Airport to cater to the increasing passenger traffic of the low cost airlines, namely Malaysia's home-grown budget airline, AirAsia. AirAsia uses Kuala Lumpur as its hub, operating flights within Malaysia and also to South East Asia and China. Air Asia's subsidiary, Air Asia X commenced long-haul services to selected destinations with effect from July 2007. Visit www.airasia.com for further details.

On arrival, you can choose to journey to Kuala Lumpur city centre by taxi, bus or high-speed train. There are also car rentals available at the airport but driving into Kuala Lumpur can be extremely taxing due to frequent traffic congestions, confusing road signs and one-way streets. Also disconcerting is Malaysia's dubious honour of having one of the highest road accident rates in the world. Reckless drivers that get almost suicidal after driving in KL's heavy traffic may leave you white-knuckled from clutching the wheel so hard.

Taxis

Taxis are the most convenient choice, bringing you directly to wherever you need to be within Kuala Lumpur city. Only selected airport taxis are allowed to ferry passengers from KLIA to Kuala Lumpur. Operating on a prepaid basis, prices are fixed based on various districts within KL and its surrounds. You can pay for your journey at the designated 'Airport Limo' booths by specifying the destination, collecting the receipt and hopping into any of the waiting taxis. Avoid incessant

3

touts that hang out in the arrival foyer, even when they seem to show you 'legitimate' lists of their prices. The normal 'budget' Airport Limo fare to the city centre (Petronas Twin Tower, for instance) was last priced at RM67.40. For a 'premium' rate, you can also upgrade to a limousine service but when travelling alone, going 'budget' is perfectly fine. The journey takes approximately 45 minutes, depending on traffic conditions. For the return journey, you can take any taxi from the city but a note of advice for all taxi journeys in Malaysia: although taxis are required to charge by metered fare, always ask if the journey is 'metered' or else agree on the price first, preferably even before you climb in.

Trains

If you need to get into KL in a fast, reliable manner, then the comfortable KLIA Ekspres is highly recommended. Trains depart at 15-minute intervals; the non-stop journey between KL Sentral and KLIA takes only 28 minutes and costs RM35. There is also another train that has three intermediate stops called KL Transit that takes you to Sepang town centre, Putrajaya, Cyberjaya and Bandar Tasik Selatan station, where you can connect to inner city light rail (STAR LRT) and regional commuter trains (KTM).

A prepaid bus service also operates an express route from the airport to a city terminal on Jalan Duta in Kuala Lumpur. A number of public buses also provide shuttles between Kuala Lumpur and KLIA.

For more information, log on to www.klia.com.my or www.kliaekspres.com

Land

You can also enter Malaysia by road or rail from Singapore and Thailand. There are five border crossings located in the north, connecting with Thailand and two bridge crossings located in the south, leading in and out Singapore. Non-stop travel through the three countries by land will take approximately eight hours. There are several companies that provide coach services that ply the route. You can also take the regional KTM commuter trains or splurge out on luxury nostalgia by taking the Orient Express that goes from Singapore to Bangkok via Kuala Lumpur and Butterworth.

3

Traffic congestion

If you are planning to drive, be warned that the Johor-Singapore causeways are notorious for their epic traffic jams especially during peak hours, weekends and public holidays. The monthly average of travellers and vehicles crossing the checkpoints reach 8 million and 3 million respectively. It has been reported that it took drivers more than four hours to clear the slightly over one-kilometre long Johor Baru-Woodlands Causeway on a Sunday after a long weekend public holiday in Singapore. If you do intend to brave the journey, you can check traffic conditions online at www.onemotoring.com.sg, click on Woodlands or Tuas Checkpoint for updated traffic camera images.

Sea

Generally speaking, it is not often that you enter Malaysia by sea but, if you do, there are various seaports around the country that have customs and immigration facilities to enable passengers to travel between Malaysia and the neighbouring countries like Brunei Darussalam, Indonesia, Philippines, Singapore and Thailand. Cruise liners have extensive docking facilities at Kijal (Terengganu), Kota Kinabalu, Langkawi, Penang and Port Klang. You can find out more about authorised immigration entry points by sea on the Immigration Department of Malaysia's website at www.imi.gov.my

Trade missions

Every year hundreds of delegates from foreign companies travel to Malaysia on trade missions organised or supported by national agencies in their own countries. These are an excellent way for new or inexperienced exporters to test markets, attract customers, appoint agents and distributors and, of course, to make sales. There are many practical advantages to joining a trade mission – travel subsidies, prearranged flights, hotels, transfers, visa and even interpreters. While the companies have time to visit potential clients and contacts there may also be group events such as a reception at the local embassy or consulate to which the missioners can invite potential clients. Such events provide excellent opportunities for you to impress your clients or to meet local contacts socially to establish relations and credentials.

To find out about outgoing trade missions, contact the ministries, national agencies or business councils that promote trade and development in your country, such as UKTI or the US Department of Commerce, and ask to be informed about their trade missions. Business people in the UK, for instance, can visit www.link2exports.co.uk and click on Trade Missions for the country of their choice. Austrade, which is a portfolio agency under the Australian Government Department of Foreign Affairs and Trade, also maintains an up-to-date listing of international events and missions at www.austrade.gov.au The European Commission External Trade Department is an immensely rich source of information and also maintains an events calendar at www.ec.europa.eu

Health and insurance

Generally, the standard of medical facilities in Malaysia is high in major cities but can be limited in rural areas. Many doctors have been trained in reputable overseas institutions and both doctors and nursing staff will usually speak English. Most common medicines are directly available from the clinics or hospitals, while prescriptions are dispensed by trained pharmacists in pharmacies that can be found in most shopping centres.

Subsidised public healthcare is available from government clinics and hospitals but only Malaysian citizens are eligible. Private medical care is available in all major cities for foreigners and the many Malaysians who opt for it. It is acceptable to approach private specialists or hospitals directly without a GP referral. Private clinics and hospitals in Malaysia are of international standards but naturally it comes at a price. Most private hospitals require a cash deposit or a confirmation of insurance prior to admission and expect immediate payment for services. Visitors are therefore strongly advised to take up a comprehensive travel or overseas medical insurance that covers all eventualities.

There is also a growing Medical Tourism sector, which received more than 340,000 foreign visitors seeking medical treatment in Malaysia in 2007 alone. Many come for treatments and surgery that would require a long

3

Health

wait or are too expensive in their home country. There are currently 35 private hospitals, mainly located in Kuala Lumpur, Seremban, Penang and Johor Baru that are approved and licensed by the Ministry of Health. You can even take up a "Lifestyle Healthcare Packaged Tour" which combines medical treatment and a recuperation holiday in the form of a spa or resort stay. For more information and listing of approved hospitals, visit the Tourism Malaysia website: www.tourismmalaysia.com or the Malaysia Healthcare Travel website: www.malaysiahealthcare.com

Some tropical illnesses still plague the rural areas in Malaysia and it is important to seek up-to-date medical advice regarding any recommended vaccinations before travelling. Tuberculosis, hepatitis A and B are common, as is dengue fever, for which there is no vaccination or immunisation. Malaria is only a risk if you venture deep into the jungle areas.

Dehydration, sunburn and heatstroke are common due to the hot climate. Proper care should be taken to ensure that you have plenty to drink, are well protected against the sun's effects and minimise prolonged periods in the sun. Pack a suitable wardrobe of light, absorbent clothing like cotton tops and T-shirts. A light jacket, sweater, cardigan or shawl may also come in handy when spending time in the (almost always) air-conditioned indoors. It can get surprisingly chilly.

Food hygiene standards are generally high in Malaysia and those involved in food preparation are subject to Health Ministry controls. Food handlers undergo regular screening against diseases. Nevertheless, it is important to observe common sense when selecting somewhere to dine – if eating from outdoor stalls, ensure that they are clean and that the food is freshly prepared.

At certain times of the year, smoke haze, caused by forest fires, can reduce both air quality and visibility in most parts of Malaysia, including Kuala Lumpur. Those with respiratory conditions should take special precautions by staying indoors or carrying an inhaler at all times.

For the latest updates on health advice, check with your country's Foreign Office before your travel.

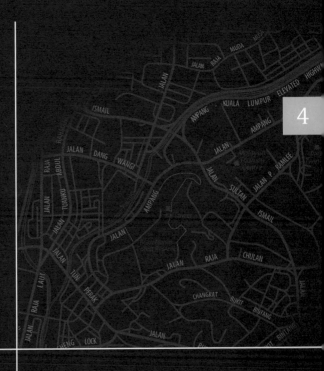

4

the ground rules

the ground rules

This section takes the reader by
the hand and talks through the
nitty-gritty of everyday life, from
how to get around to how much
to tip the bell-boy. Knowledge
of these essentials provides the
confidence to go out and do
business effectively.

Currency

The local currency is called Ringgit Malaysia (RM). The peg against the US Dollar, imposed during the financial crisis of 1998, was lifted in 2005. However, at the time of writing, the capital control measure is still in place. Non-residents are required to declare on custom forms issued when bringing into Malaysia more than US$2,500, including traveller's cheques. Upon departure, non-residents must declare and obtain permission to leave the country with funds exceeding RM1,000.

Ringgit banknotes are issued in the following denominations RM1, RM2, RM5, RM10, RM50, RM100 and RM500 while coins are issued in one sen, five sen, 10 sen, 20 sen, 50 sen and RM1 denominations.

If you have foreign currencies, exchanging them when you arrive in Malaysia usually gives you a better deal than doing so in your home country. Banks and hotels are also mostly willing to exchange foreign currencies but you get a much better rate from money exchange kiosks in many of the town centres. Some major departmental stores are also willing to accept foreign currencies at a fixed exchange rate, usually lower than that offered in the exchange market.

Banking

Banking facilities are easily accessible in Malaysia and there are several reputable local institutions as well as international players that can cater to your banking needs. Foreign currency and traveller's cheques can be converted into ringgit at banks or authorised money changers throughout the country. There is an abundance of Automated Teller Machines (ATMs) all over Malaysia. Just walk into any of the large shopping centres and you will most likely find an ATM or money exchange.

Given the capital control in place, it is best to withdraw local currency when you are in Malaysia (at the airport, for instance), using an internationally accepted debit card (such as Cirrus or PLUS). Almost all of the major Malaysian banks' ATMs will accept these debit cards. Credit card usage is widely accepted in Malaysia except

4

in small businesses. Some smaller stores may also impose a minimum-spending amount before credit cards are accepted. Some of the major local banks are Alliance Bank Bhd, Hong Leong Bank Bhd, Malaya Bank Bhd (or Maybank), Public Bank Bhd and RHB Banking Group. Foreign banks with a strong presence in Malaysia include Citibank, Deutsche Bank, HSBC, Standard Chartered Bank and Royal Bank of Scotland (RBS).

You can find a full listing of banks in Malaysia by visiting the Central Bank of Malaysia (Bank Negara Malaysia) at www.bnm.gov.my

Tipping

Tipping is not common practice in restaurants or when taking taxis in Malaysia unless you found the service to be impeccable. Most restaurants charge a 10% service charge to your bill so any tips would be in addition to that. A typical situation in which tipping may be appropriate is when you are dining with a large group in a high-end restaurant. In this instance, a RM5 or RM10 tip is usually sufficient. Hotel porters usually expect a tip of more than RM2.

Getting Around
By air

It is easy to travel within Malaysia by air because most of Malaysia's state capitals have their own airports. But it rarely makes much sense to fly within Peninsular Malaysia as most journeys take as much time to travel by air as by overland, especially if you consider the journey time from point to point. If you do fly domestically, you can consider flying with Malaysia Airlines (www.malaysiaairlines.com) or AirAsia (www.airasia.com). Malaysia Airlines has also recently introduced Fireflyz, a wholly-owned subsidiary that offers budget flights within Malaysia and Asia (www.fireflyz.com.my). Private carriers, such as Berjaya Air, provide services to several island getaways in Malaysia (www.berjayaair.com).

4

By sea

There are many islands around Malaysia that are only accessible by scheduled or charter ferry services. These islands are usually idyllic getaways and are popular with locals and visitors alike. Some of the notable island resorts in Malaysia are Penang, Langkawi, Pangkor, Tioman, Redang, Pulau Perhentian, Pulau Besar and Labuan. Each of these islands has different ferry departure points.

Fast boats and small river crafts are a popular way of getting about in Sabah and Sarawak, especially to the more isolated settlements. Cruise ships ply between the major port of Port Klang and destinations in Thailand and Singapore as well as provide overnight cruises to the island of Penang. For information on how to get to some of the above islands, ferry operators and cruise ships, log on to www.tourism.gov.my

By land

Peninsular Malaysia is well serviced by the North-South Highway, East-Coast Highway and the Kuala Lumpur-Kuantan Highway, which link up coastal roads and the rest of the road systems in the country. The legal speed limit on these highways is 110 kilometres per hour. The highways are managed by PLUS Sdn Bhd and a toll is charged based on the distance travelled. You can pay for the toll charges with cash at all tollbooths located at each highway exit. There is also a network of highways and roads connecting the major towns in Sabah and Sarawak.

Car rental

Foreign visitors travelling with time-critical agendas are recommended to hire a driver with car rental. This can usually be arranged through any of the reputable hotels. Car rental can also be arranged directly from Avis, Sixt or Budget and is recommended when you have meetings in several locations that are slightly away from the main towns (such as in designated industrial parks and trade zones).

4

Taxis

Taxis in major cities are usually fitted with meters. In KL, the rate is currently RM2 for the first two kilometres and 10 sen for every subsequent 200 metres for a normal red and white taxi. However, a surcharge of 50% will be levied between midnight and 6 a.m. Premium taxis are bright yellow in colour and are priced higher. Demand often outstrips supply when in comes to taxis during the peak periods. This is when your haggling skills will come in handy. If you flag down a taxi during rush hour, the driver may turn down the fare due to 'traffic jam' where you are headed. Offer to pay him a flat fee (more than RM7 for short and more than RM10 for longer journeys) instead of using the meter and he will most likely comply, unless there really is bad congestion en route. In which case, you may be expected to up the ante even further. The rule of thumb of more than RM7 for short journeys and more than RM10 for longer journeys also applies to smaller Malaysian towns. If you are unsure of the distance to your destination, ask a few taxi-drivers to state their price and bargain until you can settle on a price.

Interstate taxi rides are also charged at a fixed rate and it's best to settle on a price before getting into the taxi. As a gauge, the 4-hour journey from Kuala Lumpur to Johor Baru costs around RM250. These taxis are usually found at the main bus terminals in most major towns.

Buses

By far the most economical and comfortable way to travel interstate, bus services are readily available and operate between all major cities and towns in Peninsular Malaysia as well as to Singapore and Thailand. Buses travelling between major cities and towns tend to be mostly air-conditioned. Some of these coaches are marketed as business class or executive coaches and offer a higher level of service and comfort. There are also similar services operating in East Malaysia.

The only downside to travelling by bus is the difficulty in obtaining relevant information to plan your journeys. To get information or buy tickets, you need to go down to the bus terminal to find the schedule and book tickets. In Kuala Lumpur, for example, there are four bus terminals

4

– Puduraya Bus Station, Putra Pekeliling Bus Station (Hentian Putra Pekeliling), Duta Bus Station (Hentian Duta) and Old Town Petaling Jaya. All of them are overcrowded and confusing. In addition, there are many other spots around the city where some bus companies sell their tickets and where their bus arrival and depart from. Fortunately, departures are frequent, so you do not need to make advance reservations on most routes except prior to major public holidays.

There are extensive routes and endless permutations of destinations offered by the bus companies. Some of the recommended bus companies are featured here to help those wishing to explore Malaysia by coach. Travellers wanting to escape the chaotic madness of the four main bus terminals in Kuala Lumpur should pay attention to the alternative terminals that service the 'executive' or 'luxury' coaches.

Transnational Ekspress – The national interstate bus operator operates from Puduraya Bus Station and Duta Bus station and offers express services to most major cities in Malaysia www.nadi.com.my/transportation

Plusliner – Another major bus operator in Malaysia that offers express routes to Perlis, Kedah, Butterworth, Ipoh & Johor and Singapore leaving from Puduraya Bus Station. It offers luxury coaches under the 'Nice' branding that leaves from the Old Railway Station on Jalan Sultan Hishamudin, Kuala Lumpur to Singapore, with an option to drop off in Johor Bahru or in Penang. www.plusliner.com

First Coach – Offers exclusive service from Kuala Lumpur to Singapore. Although less luxurious than others in this class, it offers unbeatable convenience due to its arrival and departure points that are within walking distance from MRT/LRT stations. In Kuala Lumpur, the terminal is at Jalan Kamuja in Bangsar Utama, about 100m from the Bangsar PUTRA LRT station. In Singapore, passengers are dropped off at Novena Square, next to the Novena MRT station.

Tel: +65 6822 2111 (Singapore) 3 2287 3311
       (Malaysia)

4

Rail

The national railway, Malaysia Keretapi Tanah Melayu (KTM), operates a domestic train service that dates back to the British colonial era. Though a picturesque journey through the smaller towns and countryside, it is not a time-efficient mode of transport. The main north-south rail line passes through Johor Bahru, Kuala Lumpur, Ipoh, Arau and Padang Besar. The East Coast service branches from the main line at Gemas in Negeri Sembilan and terminates at Tumpat in Kelantan. Fares are very affordable and the booths are air-conditioned, comfortable, albeit slightly rundown. You can buy tickets at any of stations located mostly in town and city centres. In Kuala Lumpur, the main railway station is located at Jalan Sultan Hishamudin and is one of the oldest and grandest train stations in Malaysia (www.ktmb.com.my).

Inner-city rail

Kuala Lumpur's public transport system is made up of three Light Rail Transit (LRT) lines, the semicircular Monorail and the KTM Komuter trains that journey to the surrounding suburbs. It is a concerted effort to ease the traffic situation in KL and offer commuters a good transport alternative but it still leaves much to be improved.

That said, fares are cheap and it remains the most effective way to get around central Kuala Lumpur, especially during peak hours and rainy days (when taxis are scarce). All public transport in KL, excluding the airport express, accepts payment in the form of the Touch 'n Go card. These cards can be purchased at major stations for a minimum stored value of RM10 (additional RM10 as refundable deposit).

Communications

Post

Post Malaysia is the main postal service provider, operating 650 offices all around Malaysia. For many Malaysians, a visit to the post office conjures up images of waiting in a long line in a stuffy and overcrowded room. The postal service is slow and service standards are just acceptable. Nevertheless, they can be relied on to send non-urgent mail at a low rate. The government is currently trying to overhaul the postal service by injecting investments to improve service standards and efficiency.

Thankfully, there are many international courier services that can help fill the gap. International courier companies like UPS, Fedex, TNT and DHL all have offices in towns and cities to provide fast, reliable services. For local mail, you can also use local courier services such as City-link or Nationwide Express.

Courier firms

4

City-Link Global Network
www.citylinkexpress.com
Tel: 3 5033 3800

DHL Worldwide Express Malaysia
www.dhl.com.my
Tel: 1800 888 388 or 3 7964 2800

Fedex Express Malaysia
www.fedex.com/my
Tel: 1800 88 6363 or 3 2179 0370

Nationwide Express
www.nationwide2u.com
Tel: 3 5512 7000

TNT Express Worldwide
www.tnt.com
Tel: 1300 882 882 or 3 7962 2929

UPS Malaysia – United Parcel Service
www.ups.com
Tel: 3 7784 1233

Internet
Internet subscription has increased dramatically over the last few years and is expected to exceed 60% of the population in 2008. Broadband Internet is now also widely available. Internet cafes can easily be found in KL and major towns, although you might encounter more teenage cyber-gamers than backpackers in them. Many hotels in Malaysia, especially in KL, offer Internet access in their rooms, mostly at a high daily charge. There is,

4

however, a growing trend for these hotels to offer free Wi-Fi access in their lobbies, so it is useful to ask when you check in. In addition, you may also find many shopping centres and cafes that offer Wi-Fi hotspots or sometimes even free Wi-Fi access. If you own a laptop, the Maxis WLAN service is the best deal around for mobile surfing. For RM15, a prepaid card allows you to get unlimited usage for 14 days in conveniently located, designated Wi-Fi hot spots. Ask for WLAN Prepaid at any authorised Maxis stores (there is one located in KLCC).

Internet providers

TMNET   –   www.streamyx.com.my
                     Tel: 1300 881 515 / 1300 889 515

Jaring   –   www.jaring.my
                     Tel: 3 8991 7080

Celcom   –   www.celcom.com.my
                     Tel: 3 3630 8888

Maxis   –   www.maxis.com.my
                     Tel: 1800 828 998

Telephone

The international dialling code for Malaysia is 60. Malaysian landline telephone numbers have either seven or eight digits. There is also a two- or three-digit area code prefix that needs to be added when dialling from outside the area. The area codes are:

02	–	Singapore
03	–	Kuala Lumpur, Putrajaya, Selangor
04	–	Penang, Perlis, Kedah
05	–	Perak
06	–	Negeri Sembilan, Malacca
07	–	Johor
087/088	–	Sabah
082/083	–	Sarawak
09	–	Pahang, Terengganu, Kelantan

Mobile phones have prefix codes such as 012, 013, 016, 017 and 019 that correspond to a different mobile phone provider. Area codes are not required when calling a number of the same area code from a landline.

However, it is mandatory when calling from a mobile phone. 1300 prefix means that calls are charged as a local call and 1800 prefix calls are free from landlines and charged as a local call when dialled from a mobile phone. To dial internationally, the access code is 00, followed by country code, area code and lastly the telephone number. The same is true when dialling from a mobile phone – 00 or the '+' prefix.

The **emergency number** is **999** and can be dialled from any phone, free of charge. For Directory Assistance, dial 103; for International Directory Assistance, dial 108.

Mobile phones

Malaysia has three mobile phone providers – Maxis, DiGi and Celcom. Mobile networks utilise the GSM 900 and 1800 systems. Coverage is generally high in more built-up towns and cities and can get a little problematic when visiting the small villages or the more secluded islands.

If you are travelling with a phone that does not enable international roaming, you can easily buy a local pre-paid SIM card that enables you to make IDD calls; or if you are planning to travel to the neighbouring countries, then opt for a prepaid card that allows international roaming. These cards can be found in convenience stores across the country (7-Eleven stores or convenience stores at selected petrol stations) or at the authorised dealers found in the shopping malls.

The default **emergency number for GSM mobile phones**, is **112**, and can be used even without a SIM card. Calls to 112 will be routed to emergency call centres.

Television

There are currently six free-to-air channels available on Malaysian television and they offer an array of programmes in the various spoken languages – Malay, English, Mandarin, Cantonese and Tamil. Of these, RTM1 and RTM2 are state-owned channels, while TV3, ntv7, 8TV and TV9 are privately-owned channels that feature more English and up-to-date programming.

4

For the latest international news, latest American series and blockbuster movies, you can tune in to Malaysia's most popular satellite network which is available pay-to-view – Astro. Many of the hotels feature Astro, which brings you news channels such as BBC, CNN, CNBC, and Channel New Asia.

Radio

There are 21 government-owned radio stations in Malaysia and 23 privately-owned stations. Frequencies vary from state to state and you can find stations that broadcast in each of the spoken language in Malaysia. Some of the English stations for Kuala Lumpur and the Klang Valley are Hitz FM (92.9), Fly FM (95.8) and Capital FM (88.9).

Newspapers and magazines

Malaysia's news publications are highly influenced by the government and the ruling coalition's political parties. The two major English newspapers are good examples of this. The *Star* is the most popular English newspaper and appears in a tabloid format. It is majority-owned by the Malaysian Chinese Association, the second largest political party in the Barisan Nasional alliance. The *New Straits Times*, its closest competitor, is owned by Prima Media, which is in turn owned by a holding company linked to the ruling party, UMNO. Prima Media is, in fact, the largest media group in Malaysia, owning most of the private television stations and radio, and has a 59% share total of print advertising through its publications that also include The *Malay Mail* and *Berita Harian*.

Utusan Malaysia and *Berita Harian* are the two major newspapers published in Bahasa Malaysia and are both in favour of UMNO's politics. *Sin Chew Daily* and *China Press* are the main Chinese dailies while The *Makkal Osai* and *Malaysia Nanban* are published in Tamil for the Indian community in Malaysia.

Foreign press such as *International Herald Tribune* (IHT) and *Asian Wall Street Journal* (AWSJ) are also readily available in Malaysia. If it is 'on the ground' business news you are after, check out the local weekly business

4

publication, *The Edge*. It provides up-to-date information about the Malaysian financial market and is an excellent source of local business insights. *Far Eastern Economic Review* is a monthly that looks not just at Malaysia's economy but also provides views of the region that Malaysia is intrinsically linked to.

Language

The official language is Malay or Bahasa Malaysia, whose root can easily be traced to the Indonesian language (Bahasa Indonesia). The language is essentially an amalgamation of Sanskrit, Hindi, Tamil, Arab, Portuguese, Spanish, English and even some Chinese dialects. Being the medium of instruction in national schools, Malay is spoken by all Malaysians of all races.

English

A legacy of the British colonial rule, English is also taught as a second language in all schools and is widely spoken in urban areas. However, most Malaysians, interacting amongst themselves, favour a form of colloquial English that not only stretches the rules of grammar but is also a colourful mix (or "rojak") of Malay, Chinese and Tamil phrases. Though it can prove to be a challenge for other English-speakers to understand, it can also serve to be a great conversation starter. Malaysians generally love to "teach" you or explain the origins of some of these "Manglish" phrases to you (try "rojak").

Within the ethnic Chinese communities, Cantonese, Hokkien, Hakka and Teochew are the main groups that migrated from southern China generations ago. Each group has its own dialect, which is still widely spoken. In addition to the dialect they learnt from home, many Chinese also speak and read Mandarin, particularly those who attended Chinese schools, as it is the medium of instruction there. This makes them trilingual or multilingual in four languages. Correspondingly, there are also some Chinese who were in Malay-medium or English-medium schools that cannot understand a word of Mandarin or any of the dialects. The same can also be true of Indians with their own language.

4

Tamil and Malayalam are the main Indian languages spoken by the Indian community as their ancestors were mostly from the southern states of Tamil Nadu and Kerala in India. There is also a sizeable group in the Punjabi community that speaks Punjabi.

In Sabah and Sarawak, the different tribes there speak different languages within their own communities. The Kadazan-Dusun tribe is the largest in Sabah, while the Iban tribe is the biggest group in Sarawak.

Working hours

Normal working hours in Malaysia are consistent with the eight-hour working day, and all government offices and banks now operate a five day-week. Some local business offices may open on Saturdays for half a day in the morning and retail outlets are open throughout the week, including Saturdays and Sundays, and are closed only on major public holidays.

However, the states of Kelantan, Terengganu and Kedah practice different work hours. Sundays to Thursdays are full working days. Friday is the Islamic day of rest so the 'weekend' is Friday and Saturday.

Working hours in Kelantan, Terengganu and Kedah states:

For government offices
8.00 a.m. to 4.45 p.m. (from Sundays to Wednesdays)
8.00 a.m. to 4.30 p.m. (on Thursdays)

For banks
9.30 a.m. to 4.00 p.m. (from Sundays to Thursdays)

Working hours in all other states:
For government offices
8.00 a.m. to 5.30 p.m. (from Mondays to Fridays)

For banks
9.30 a.m. to 4.00 p.m. (from Mondays to Fridays)

Private offices are open from 9 a.m. to 5 p.m. (Monday-Friday) and 9 a.m. to 1 p.m. (Saturday, if applicable). Retail hours for departmental stores are generally 10 a.m. to 10 p.m., seven days a week.

Islam in the corporate world

4

The majority of the population are ethnic Malays and their religion is Islam. Though religious beliefs do not play a main role in the corporate world, religious duties, such as praying five times daily, are still performed throughout the working day. Prayers are conducted in "Surau" (prayer rooms), which can be found in most offices, public buildings and shopping centres when mosques are too far away. Friday afternoon is the weekly prayer time at the mosque and all Muslims are officially excused from office for two and a half hours anytime between 12 p.m. and 3 p.m. Some provinces observe Friday as the day of rest and close for business. Kuala Lumpur maintains a more western weekly pattern.

Ramadan, the month of fasting, is strictly observed. It is worthwhile knowing when Ramadan is each year, since it is based on the Islamic calendar. Government departments often find themselves understaffed at this time, making the processing of visas and other official business somewhat tardy. Manufacturing, building and construction tend to slow down during this month as well. Lunch meetings should be avoided and offers of drinks or food should also be avoided during this time when dealing with Malay counterparts.

Ramadan

Islamic law forbids the paying or collection of interest by its followers. So, since the 1960s, Malaysian financial institutions have offered Islamic Banking based on the framework that Islamic banks have already established in the Middle East. Islamic banking carries out banking business similar to that of commercial banks but its banking products comply with the principles of Syariah (or Islamic) law. For example, the bank offers deposit-taking products such as current and savings deposit under the concept of Al-Wadiah Yad Dhamanah (guaranteed custody), investment deposits under the concept of Al-Mudharabah (profit-sharing) and house

Islamic law

Islamic banking

financing under Bai' Bithaman Ajil (deferred payment sale). Islamic banking does not affect non-Muslim and commercial or business transactions and is usually only offered at the personal banking level.

Public Holidays and Events

There are eleven days of public holiday mandated by the Malaysian government. However, under the Labour Law, private companies can pick from the gazetted public holiday list, which includes some compulsory public holidays. Sounds confusing? Well, most companies will generally choose the major festivals and weigh out the remaining options with the wishes of its workforce. The more commonly celebrated public holidays in 2009 are:

Hari Raya Puasa (End of fasting month):	20 Sep*
Chinese New Year:	26 Jan
Workers' Day:	1 May
Birthday of Yang di-Pertuan Agong: (Supreme Head of State)	6 June
Hari Raya Haji:	27 Nov*
Awal Muharram:	18 Dec*
National Day:	31 Aug
Birthday of Prophet Muhammad:	9 Mar*
Deepavali:	17 Oct
Christmas Day:	25 Dec
Hari Raya Haji:	27 Nov
Wesak Day:	9 May

*Dates are subject to change, depending on the lunar reading.

For Chinese New Year and Hari Raya Puasa, employers, especially those in the manufacturing sector, may choose to extend the holiday, sometimes into weeks. Take care to check with your local contacts during these periods and get an update of when they resume business.

Other notable festivals celebrated by the various ethnic groups of Malaysia are listed here. Even though they are not public holidays, there are usually celebrations in full swing, one way or another.

Mid-Autumn Festival – Alternatively known as the Moon Festival, Lantern Festival or Mooncake Festival, the Mid-Autumn Festival is held on the full moon day (15th day) of the eighth month of the Chinese calendar. In 2009 it will be on 3 October.

Thaipusam – An annual Hindu festival commemorating the birthday of Lord Murugan. Over a million devotees and visitors throng Batu Caves on this eventful celebration every year. In 2009 it will occur on 10 January.

Kaamatan (Sabah) – A harvest festival celebrated by the Kadazan people of Sabah on 30 and 31 May each year.

Gawai Dayak (Sarawak) – A thanksgiving day marking good harvest, held on 1 June yearly in Sarawak. Iban and Bidayuh dress in their colourful costumes to make ceremonial offerings of traditional delicacies and *tuak* (home-made rice wine) to the gods of rice and prosperity.

Events

Malaysia plays host to an exciting range of events and some of the highlights are listed below:

Sporting

Formula 1 Malaysian Grand Prix – www.malaysiangp.com.my
Tour de Langkawi – www.tdl.com.my
Kuala Lumpur International Marathon – www.klmarathon.gov.my
Penang Bridge International Marathon – www.penangmarathon.llmnet.gov.my
Penang Internation Dragon Boat Race – www.penangdragonboat.com

Others

Merdeka Day Celebration – 31 August
Rainforest World Music Festival – www.rainforestmusic-borneo.com
Malaysia Mega Sale Carnival – www.malaysiamegasale.com.my
Langkawi International Maritime and Aerospace (LIMA) Exhibition – www.limamaritime.com.my

4

Social customs

Malaysia is a multicultural society, and social etiquette should, by right, differ accordingly. However, centuries of living together and integration mean that everyone, more or less, practise, some social customs as though they were their own. Some of these common courtesies and customs are as follows:

Except in large cities like Kuala Lumpur, most ladies avoid dressing too revealingly or provocatively. Although the more liberal form of dress will not get a tourist into any form of trouble legally, travellers are generally advised to adopt a more conservative dress code, especially when visiting public building and places of worship. Locals dress casually during non-office hours. Whether going out for a nice dinner or a social function, ladies usually don smart jeans or slacks paired with a nice top and choose stylish simple dresses over red-carpet gowns. Men are usually seen in jeans or Bermuda shorts but will sometimes dress up for clubs and bars that prohibit sandals, sneakers or jeans.

Alcohol and pork are forbidden in Islam so take care when going out with Malaysians who are Muslims. Do not offer them the forbidden items and avoid establishments that are non-halal, although these really are few and far between. Some of the locals may eat with their hands, though you should not feel obliged to do the same; but, if you wish to do so, always remember to eat only with your right hand. The right hand should also always be extended for a handshake or to present and receive a gift/offering. More on hands, pointing with an extended index finger is considered rude. Use the whole extended hand with palm up to indicate the subject instead. Or try to identify and imitate the 'closed fist with curled index finger under the extended thumb' manoeuvre if you can.

Malaysians have a more conservative attitude towards physical contact compared to the west. Parents rarely hug their children, even in private, but rather show their affections through socially or religiously prescribed gestures. With this in mind, touching a stranger is not done except for handshakes. The head is spiritually revered and should not be touched, especially not by strangers, so refrain from patting a child on the head. From the head, we now move to the feet. It is considered extremely rude to point with or show anyone the soles of your feet. So do not rest your ankles on your knees, or the person sitting next to you will feel very offended indeed.

4

Physical signs of affection in public are rarely displayed by the locals, so, especially in the provincial towns, it may be frowned upon. While Malaysians may not appreciate the signs of intimacy, they are more than happy to discuss seemingly intimate details that you prefer keep to yourself such as your age, weight, marital status or even income. Graciously avoid the questions if you would rather not answer, but Malaysians appreciate some degree of candidness in this respect and you can usually count on them to reciprocate with their own answers. Another demonstration of this characteristic is this: anyone who is older than 18 maybe addressed as "Uncle/Auntie" or "Pakcik/Makcik" by someone younger. So you may find yourself introduced as Uncle So-and-So or Auntie So-and-So to any children. This establishes you with the "elder" status, to which respect is due.

Malaysians usually go barefoot at home, so, if you are invited to someone's home, always remove your shoes before or just after the door. Think of it this way, Muslims remove their shoes before entering a mosque and so do Hindus at their temples, so it is a nice gesture and a show of respect to remove your shoes upon entering someone's house. If you would like to present a gift as well, then you generally will not go wrong with chocolates, confectionery or a souvenir from your country. Avoid anything sharp (knives, scissors or cutters) and choose a brightly coloured gift-wrap whenever possible. Malay Muslims consider dogs unclean and are not allowed to touch them so you will not find them in Muslim homes. Keep in mind that when you feel the urge to pat a dog in public, do not do it in front of your Malay counterparts. Or else stop wondering why they have been keeping their distance.

Through interacting with Malaysians, you will discover that they greatly value courtesy and are always striving

4

to be respectful in their daily dealings with people. If you emulate these values, even when you make a major social gaffe, they will whole-heartedly overlook that with a smile (and remember to return that smile too).

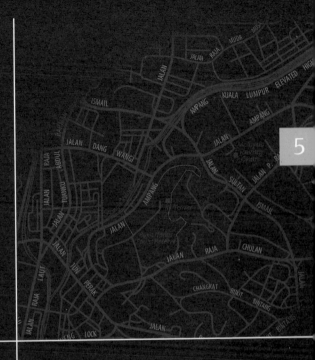

5

getting down
to business

getting down
to business

This chapter provides elementary
guidance on the etiquette of business,
and also contains details of useful local
organisations who can assist with the
more complicated requirements of
business transactions.

Business culture

Business travellers may at first perceive the multi-ethnic population in Malaysia as a minefield of cultural sensitivities at first. However, many discover that Malaysia is generally a relaxed place and are surprised by the warmth of Malaysians – be it the Malays, Chinese, Indians or anyone who considers themselves Malaysians. This is a society that values tolerance, respect for one another, peace and harmony. Visitors will find their cultural blunders generally tolerated or graciously overlooked, but a savvy foreigner who is conversant in Malaysian business practices and local customs can send the right signals to help break down the initial reserve.

Although the business culture in Malaysia does not differ fundamentally from the international standards, business tends to be conducted more on the basis of personal relationships or rapport. It takes time to establish trust and legitimacy with local contacts. Hard sell and readiness to challenge rarely see results here. Doing business in Malaysia requires commitment to a long-term effort and you will need to invest time and money to visit regularly and develop a good rapport with clients, agents and other business contacts.

Even though Bahasa Malaysia is the official language, English is widely spoken, particularly in major cities; so do not hesitate to pick up the phone for general enquiries and initial contact making. Many Malaysians are engaged in international business and are becoming more westernised due to their overseas education or experiences working abroad. With the gentlest of probing, a Malaysian business contact may happily divulge that he studied in a university in America, has a sister living in England and spends his holiday skiing in Japan. Yet, with this air of internationalism, it is useful to remember that each of the three main ethnic groups of Malaysia (Malay, Chinese and Indian) is religiously and culturally distinct and should be approached accordingly.

5

5

Business etiquette
The ground work

Doing business in Malaysia is all about contacts, contacts, contacts. So, if you are new to the market, do extensive research on your targets using the database offered by your trade commissions, chambers of commerce or even Malaysia's trade and industry promotion agencies. Similarly you can also use their knowledge and expertise to find a suitable and reliable local partner/agent who can in turn pave the way and establish foundations for you. Look closely at your own business network to tap into any associates that may already have contacts in Malaysia.

Once introductions are made, take them seriously, especially if they are made by people from or representing large established corporations. Establish yourself by providing the relevant information to your target and respond to all correspondence in a timely manner. Do not be despondent if you do not see immediate buy-in. Malaysians rarely commit to anything new or untested. It may take a while to build trust but keep persisting until you find the right person to do business with. It may take several trips before you encounter any success but do not lose focus once you have committed yourself.

Appointments

Malaysian executives are quite busy and travel frequently. Hence, try to schedule appointments at least two weeks in advance. Call a day ahead or a couple of hours before the appointment to ask if the time you are expected remains unchanged. Always arrive punctually for appointments (allow extra time for traffic congestion in major cities) but do not get frustrated if your local contact is late or if the meeting is slightly delayed. The concept of appointment time may take on a more fluid meaning for some, although, generally speaking, most Malaysian firms see punctuality as good business practice.

The best times for meetings are mornings from Tuesdays to Fridays. Most firms have their internal group meetings on Mondays. If you would like an afternoon appointment, schedule it after 2 p.m. but avoid Friday afternoons altogether when dealing with a Bumiputra company. In some instances, it is perfectly acceptable for Malaysians to meet at 5:30 p.m. when the working day ends. Asian work ethics means that almost everyone works beyond the contracted hours.

It may even play to your advantage if meetings are scheduled just before mealtimes. Extending the meeting beyond the boardroom and into a more casual environment (restaurants or even after-work drinks when dealing with non-Muslim entrepreneurs) gives you an excellent opportunity and the perfect setting to build rapport and foster relationships. Inviting the junior executives may be a strategy you might want to consider, especially if they can help shed light on a meeting that ended on ambiguous terms.

Dress code

Malaysia is predominantly a Muslim country and modest dress is advisable. Business attire for male executives consist of long-sleeved business shirt and tie coupled with dark-coloured work trousers. Business jackets are normally only worn when meeting high-level executives or senior officials and, even on these occasions, it is perfectly acceptable to remove the jacket before the meeting starts. Female executives wearing business suits can do the same, but, if you intend to remove your jacket in a meeting, make sure that you are wearing a top with sleeves. Many government ministries and agencies have banned ladies with exposed shoulders from entering their premises. Needless to say, sensible hemlines are the order of the day.

Most foreigners need to climatise to Malaysia's sweltering heat. Allowing for an extra five minutes of 'cooling down' time at the meeting place will ensure that you enter the meeting looking fresh rather than as though you've just run around the tracks.

Greetings

Each ethnic group in Malaysia has their traditional greeting but, when it is a business setting, a handshake is generally acceptable for both men and women. Just in case, here are two guidelines that are widely applicable:

5 **Business cards**

When you meet with male executives, extend your right hand to them and unless they lay their hand on yours and clasp your hand (in which case you can give a normal firm handshake), or else refrain from a tight grip and proceed with an assertive shake with your hand lightly locked in position. This may sound contrary to your usual style but it is an appropriate response to an unsuspectingly limp handshake offered by some to minimise physical contact (see "Social Customs" in Chapter 4). Another reason for the limp handshake may also be because your Muslim counterpart may wish to perform a "Salam", which requires them to bring their hand to their chest after touching your hand to 'greet you from their heart'. In this case, you can also bring your right hand over your heart to return this gracious greeting.

When you meet female executives, always start with your right hand placed lightly on your left chest (heart). Only when they offer you their hand for a handshake the same procedure as the male executive applies. If the female does not extend her hand for a handshake, simply keep your hand on your chest and greet her with a smile and a slight nod.

Business cards are always exchanged at the first meeting. It does not matter if you have been to the office before; if there is someone new that you are meeting, you should exchange cards at the start of your meeting. Always check before each meeting that you have extra cards. The preferred gesture is to give and receive business cards with both hands, making sure that the card is with its text side up and turned such that the text direction faces the receiver. There is no real symbolism attached to this act except that it is courteous to present it so. It is also considered polite to read what is written on the card presented to you before keeping it neatly laid next to you on the table. Some prefer to put the card away soon after it is exchanged and read, but keeping the card handy means you can always discreetly refer to the card.

You may need to refer to the card more often than you think. Names of Malaysians can prove to be a challenge to most foreigners. To simplify, there are two things to take note of:

Correct forms of address

Malays and Indians have Arabic or Hindu names that are made up of two or three names. The last name is usually not a family name as understood by western culture. It is, in fact, the first name of the bearer's father. So Yusoff Ismail, for example, is in fact, Yusoff, son of Ismail. To correctly address him, he should be known as Mr Yusoff or Encik Yusoff. Similarly, Shankar Sivasuriyamoorthy is Mr Shankar. The same is true for Malay and Indian females. Chinese names are usually made up of three characters and most Chinese are addressed by the phonetic spelling of their Chinese name. Because the Chinese put their family name first, Tan Cheong Beng should be Mr Tan and not Mr Beng. Chinese who have a western name will place their family name after it, so Mr Tan may also be known as Vincent Tan Cheong Beng. There are exceptions, however; like Indians with Singh as their last names, (they should be addressed with both names – Mr Parneet Singh) or Indians with European-influenced ancestry (Audrey D'Souza is Miss D'Souza).

Titles

Malaysia's constitutional monarchy confers titles on citizens who have contributed to or made a significant impact on society. There are various titles given and, though some are higher ranked than the others, all of the titled individuals should be accorded deep respect. There are many titled individuals that still play an active role in the government and in private enterprises as well, so there is a high chance that you may meet with some of them. Some of these titles for male recipients are, for example Dato, Datuk, Tan Sri and Tun. Titles for a female may be given because she is a wife of a male recipient (Datin, Tok Puan, Puan Sri, Toh Puan), or she may also have been conferred one in her own right (Dato, Datuk, Datin Paduka, Tun).

Other titles include the ones for the royal family (Tengku, Tunku, Raja, Syed and Sharifah) and, for those who have completed the Islamic *Hajj* pilgrimage.

5

Names

5

Talking business

Malaysian business people are usually more reserved during their initial meetings with foreigners so you need to spend some time building up personal as well as business rapport. Take time to make some small talk to better understand each other. They would usually like to hear your impressions of the country, your travel experiences, hobbies, or just to hear you talk about football (almost the entire male population is fanatical about the English Premier League). Malaysian will appreciate you being open and honest about your opinions but do steer away from direct criticism and negative comparisons (especially between your country and Malaysia). Avoid sensitive topics such as politics, especially since many of the larger businesses are linked to the government or ruling parties. Sincerity and coming across as genuine are the impressions you should aim for at this stage.

When you meet with middle or upper management, the executives will likely bring along lower ranking staff as part of their "training". You can almost be certain that the meeting room will be occupied by more people than you first expected. This provides excellent opportunity to ascertain the organisation dynamics. During your presentation, engage with all the levels of staff wherever possible but pay more attention to the most senior person. End your presentation with a clear indication of the outcome you would like to achieve. You will find it advantageous if you position this outcome to be a "win-win" situation for both parties.

After your presentation, open the floor with questions that are crafted to show you have their best intentions in mind. Malaysians are non-confrontational so, instead of pushing a point or pushing for a decision, aim to understand their views and misgivings about reaching a decision. Listen attentively to the questions asked and also make a note of who is asking these questions. It is useful to know who are the decision-makers and who are your "allies" for future reference when planning your next strategic move. Do not lose your cool when presented with a hard situation. Avoid being too critical in your responses and instead disagree tactfully. If there are no comments or feedback ask specific questions that will get discussions going. Instead of open-ended questions like "what do you think?" or "do you have any questions?" go with "I see you are not convinced on this point, what other information can I give you to help clarify this?" Do not expect an immediate or outright answer to conclude your meeting. End your meeting with a short recapitulation of the meeting and negotiate a timeline for the decision-maker to come back to you with feedback or an answer. Communication that shows that you are willing to help, to listen and work together for mutual benefit is more likely to help you win them over than hard sell. Not only that, you would have essentially narrowed down your follow-up tasks, bringing you a step closer to your goal.

Follow up by email should be sent as soon as possible. A call report or a short summary of what was discussed and next steps should be clearly outlined. Any samples, brochures and other promised information should be sent shortly after to show your enthusiasm and commitment. After that, regular correspondence should be maintained and your perseverance will also stand you in good stead.

5

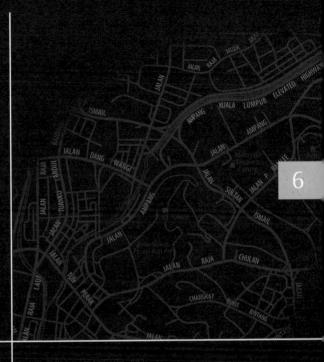

key industries

key industries

This is an overview of each
of the major industries of
the nation, and where they
stand today

Key industries

"Do not compare Singapore's economy with that of Malaysia's. It is like comparing first-class grapes (Singapore) with first-class apples (Malaysia)."

Prime Minister Datuk Seri Abdullah Ahmad Badawi
18 February 2008 *The Star*

6

Malaysia is generally regarded as one of the most successful non-Western countries to have achieved a relatively smooth transition to modern economic growth over the last century or so. The Malaysian economy has made a gargantuan leap, transforming from one based on primary commodities like tin, rubber and palm oil to an emerging multi-sector economy.

Since the 1960s, the economy has benefited from extensive restructuring with sustained growth of exports from both the primary and secondary sectors. This provided the impetus for Malaysia to become one of the fastest growing economies in the region especially in the 80s and early 90s. After the major economic shake-up of 1997, Malaysia's economic prospects now remain healthy – GDP rose 5.9% in 2007 and is on track to rise by 5-6% during 2008. Moreover, per capita income is worth approximately US$14,400 in Purchasing Power Parity terms.

Yet many of these economic accolades still pale in comparison to Singapore's achievements. Being immediate neighbours, with a long history of interdependence and rivalry, there is naturally much ground for comparison. The situation is often made more awkward when the two Asian 'tigers' meet head-to-head competing for foreign direct investments. In *CIA Factbook*, (2006) Singapore is ranked 19th while Malaysia is ranked 31st, ranked by received FDI.

Furthermore, Malaysia is also competing hard with other countries in the region. Since it is losing its price-competitiveness (especially in manufacturing) to low-wage countries like India and China, Malaysia is

6

working to improve its advantage by providing a more pro-business environment. To address this, the government has relaxed foreign ownership laws in the manufacturing sector and has also implemented a range of incentives to attract investors in priority areas such as operational headquarters, regional distribution centres and international procurement centres. The government has also invested heavily in infrastructure to facilitate both efficient business and a high standard of living, particularly in the major centres.

Industries in Malaysia are mainly located in over 200 industrial estates or parks and 13 Free Industrial Zones developed throughout the country. New sites are continuously being developed by state governments as well as private developers. Within Malaysia, the distribution of secondary industry is still distinctively unbalanced, currently heavily favouring the Peninsula, while Sabah and Sarawak are still largely dependent on primary products (timber, oil, LNG). There is an urgent need to continue the search for new industries in which Malaysia can enjoy a comparative advantage in world markets, not least because inter-ethnic harmony (as well as election votes) depends heavily on the continuance of economic prosperity.

Here is an overview of the opportunities waiting to be harvested in the various key sectors.

Electrical and electronic manufacturing

The electrical and electronics manufacturing industry is Malaysia's leading industrial sector, contributing significantly to the country's manufacturing output, exports and employment. In 2007, total gross output of the industry was RM197.1 billion (US$61.6 billion), while the industry's exports of electrical and electronics products amounted to RM266.3 billion (US$83.2 billion). This accounts for 58.9 % of Malaysia's manufactured exports and 44 % of Malaysia's total exports.

Malaysia deals mainly in electronic components, consumer electronics and industrial electronics. The biggest export group is semiconductor devices used in a diverse range of industries, such as automotive and telecommunications. Electrical products manufactured for export include household appliances, wires and cables, electrical industrial equipment, dry cells and batteries, and other electrical apparatus and supplies. Markets include Singapore, Japan and the United States.

It is a growing concern that the country has, in effect, exchanged dependence on a limited range of primary products (e.g. tin and rubber) for dependence on an equally limited range of manufactured goods, notably electronics and electronic components. Today, these industries are facing increasing competition from lower-wage countries, namely India and China. However, this may present an opportunity as well as a threat, and Malaysia's exports to these countries are also likely to grow rapidly.

6

Meanwhile, the government reacts by heavily promoting incentives to push the manufacturers to move up the value chain and to produce higher value-added products to remain competitive. There is also a significant shift in focus for research and development and the government is continuing efforts to boost demand for "Made in Malaysia" products to wean the economy off of its dependence on exports as well as gain international market share.

Contacts

Multimedia Development Corporation (MDC)
Website: www.mdc.com.my

Malaysian American Electronics Industry (MAEI)
Website: www.amcham.com.my

Malaysia Electrical & Electrronics Industry Group
(MEEIG)
Website: www.fmm.org.my

The Electrical & Electronics Association of Malaysia
(TEEAM)
Website: www.teeam.com

Computer & Multimedia Industry Association, Malaysia (PIKOM)
Website: www.pikom.org.my

Technopreners Association of Malaysia (TeAM)
Website: www.team.net.my

Malaysia Cable Manufacturers Association (MCMA)
Website: www.mcma.org.my

6

Chemicals

The chemical industry in Malaysia is mainly a resource-based sector, with a strong skew towards products related to petroleum, natural gases and palm oil (oleochemicals). Given the rich palm oil and petroleum resources of the country, Malaysia's production of oleochemicals and petrochemicals is especially advanced. In fact, Malaysia is one of the leading exporters of petrochemicals, with investments totalling RM 56.9 billion (US$ 17.5 billion) as at the end of 2007. Malaysia also has the world's largest production facility at a single location of liquefied natural gas with production capacity of 23 million metric tonnes per year.

Much of the petroleum and petrochemical production in Malaysia is managed either directly or through one of the subsidiaries of Malaysia's national oil company, Petroliam Nasional Berhad or PETRONAS, as it is commonly known. Slick and commercially-focused, PETRONAS has been recently identified as an industry role model in a 2007 *Financial Times* report of the 'New Seven Sisters'. The report charts the most influential energy companies from countries outside the Organisation for Economic Co-operation and Development.

PETRONAS

The systematic development of petrochemical zones where petrochemical plants are clustered together to create an integrated value chain has attracted big multinational brands such as BASF, BP, Dow, Shell, ExxonMobil, Eastman Chemical and Idemitsu, many of which work in successful collaboration with PETRONAS. The petrochemical zones are in Kertih (Terengganu), Gebeng (Pahang), and Pasir Gudang/Tanjung Langsat (Johor).

The current world trend to move away from traditional fuel energy to renewable energy creates tremendous growth potential for Malaysia's palm oil-related chemical industries. Palm oil has proved to be a viable biodiesel component, burgeoning demand in an industry that already is the world's largest producer and exporter of oleochemicals, accounting for about 17% of the world's output.

Other important chemical related export products in Malaysia are:

- Chemicals used in agriculture, pesticides, fertilisers
- Soap, detergent, cosmetic and toiletry preparations
- Inorganic chemicals
- Pharmaceuticals
- Paint and paint products
- Plastics products and resins

6

The plastics industry currently consists of 1,500 manufacturers and was estimated at RM16 billion in 2007. The plastics industry can be divided into seven sub-sectors, namely, packaging sub-sector, electrical & electronics sub-sector, household sub-sector, automotive sub-sector, construction sub-sector, agriculture sub-sector and others. The packaging sub-sector, both flexible and rigid (including bags, films, bottles and containers), remains the largest market for the plastic industry. The total export of plastic products was RM6.8 in 2007.

Plastics industry

Major export markets are Japan, Singapore, China, Thailand, Hong Kong, the European Union and the United States.

Contacts
Chemical Industries Council of Malaysia
Website: www.cicm.org.my

ASEAN Oleochemicals Manufacturers Group
Website: www.aomg.org.my

Malaysian Petrochemicals Association
Website: www.mpa.org.my

Petroliam Nasional Berhad (PETRONAS)
Website: www.petronas.com.my

Malaysian Plastic Manufacturers Association
Website: www.mpma.org.my

Automotive

6

The automotive industry in Malaysia was established in the early 1960s. More than forty years on, it is starting to come of age. Once hailed as another successful economic engineering project by the incumbent government leader, the industry is now poised between a protectionist past and a future that is hopefully more open to overseas competition.

Prior to the 1960s, automobiles were imported into Malaysia as completely built-up units (CBU). Local assembly of completely knocked-down (CKD) kits started in the 1960s. In 1983, Malaysia launched its first national car company – Perusahaan Otomobil Nasional or PROTON. The first PROTON car produced in 1985 was initially built on technology and parts from Mitsubishi Motors. Later models were subsequently built from local content as technology and skills have been transferred and ancillary industries were slowly developed. Early market share for PROTON car models (Saga, Wira, Waja and Perdana) reached 60% penetration, since it was the cheapest car within its class available in Malaysia. The competitive price was the result of both the low cost of domestic production as well as high import tariffs for all other non-national car makes. As of 3 August 2008, Proton has produced three million cars since 1985.

PROTON

In 1993, the second national car company – Perusahaan Otomobil Kedua or PERODUA was formed, followed by the national motorcycle project, Motosikal Dan Enjin Nasiinal Sdn Bhd or MODENAS in 1996. PERODUA produces mainly small compact cars that are badge engineered from Daihatsu. While it does not produce cars that compete in the same class or size, PERODUA has

PERODA

outsold PROTON to become the best-selling car company in Malaysia since 2006. PROTON has since tried to implement an export policy to help recover its slide at home, concentrating on other Asian markets and the Middle East.

Malaysia's government has long protected its automotive industry from foreign competition using high tariffs and non-tariff barriers. As car ownership in Malaysia nears its saturation point, the government is recognising that the protectionist policies can no longer benefit PROTON or PERODUA. The future for the automotive industry lies in integrating itself with regional and global auto and auto-parts market. The free trade agreement with ASEAN countries has opened up the established domestic automotive industry not only to competition but also to a vast regional market.

The value of component parts and accessories manufactured in the country totalled over RM 5.46 billion (US$1.61 billion) in 2007. However, there is still tremendous potential for growth as Malaysia currently imports a substantial amount of automotive components and parts, such as engines, transmissions and auto-electronic components. The total import value, including those for completely knocked-down parts, amounted to about RM9.0 billion (US$2.7 billion) during the same year.

The government would like to overcome the Malaysian automotive industry's dependency on imported parts and is wooing foreign investments in this industry sector. Foreign companies can captialise on the numerous incentives and policies provided by the government to set up local component manufacturing in Malaysia. Companies with interests in activities such as design, research and development are also sought after by policy-makers.

Even though there may still be some lingering protectionist measures, the free trade agreement is being honoured within the ASEAN region, hence opening up a large automobile and auto-parts market. With a well-established vendor network in the country, the setting-up of an export and trading base in Malaysia

6

6

for the rest of the ASEAN region and Middle East may be an opportunity also worth exploring.

Contacts
Perusahaan Otomobil Nasional Berhad (PROTON)
Website: www.proton.com.my

Perodua Sales Sdn Bhd
Website: www.perodua.com.my

MODENAS
Website: www.modenas.com.my

Malaysian Automotive Component Parts Manufacturers
Website: www.macpma.org.my

Malaysian Automotive Association
Website: www.maa.org.my

Agricultural and Food Products

Agriculture remains an important sector in Malaysia, contributing slightly over RM40 billion (approximately US$11.5 billion, 2008 forecast) to the nation's GDP. Malaysia is classified among the world's largest producers of palm oil, cocoa, pineapples, pepper and rubber. The country is also a major exporter of tropical wood. Not surprisingly, the food processing industry in Malaysia is well established and robust. Major industries include the production of refined sugar, wheat flour and baked products, non-alcoholic beverages, edible oil, dairy products, confectionery and snacks, fish and seafood products, beer, canned pineapple, and processed meat.

Small family-owned businesses or medium-sized enterprises dominate the industry, catering mostly to a small, localised market. There are also some larger companies that are listed on the Kuala Lumpur Stock Exchange as well as subsidiaries of foreign or multinational companies. These companies usually have a nationwide to regional market presence. Malaysia's processed foods are exported to more than eighty countries, with an annual export value of more than RM6 billion (US$1.9 billion). This amounts to two-thirds

of the total Malaysian food exports of over
RM10 billion.

Although the export performance of this sector has
doubled over the last ten years, Malaysia continues to
be a net importer of food products with an annual
import of more than RM15 billion (US$4.7 billion).
The government aims to increase food production –
both as raw materials and processed, making Malaysia
a net exporter in the near future.

This presents foreign companies with a large variety of
investment and growth opportunities in Malaysia.
For instance, convenience food is a large growth market
that is just being explored and developed. There are
opportunities in the food industry both in terms of
product development as well as in manufacturing
processes in Malaysia. Processed ingredients such as
additives and flavourings are mostly imported and the
government would like to encourage local production or
the setting-up of subsidiaries of foreign food processing
companies.

6

The global market for halal food is currently valued
at about US$547 billion a year. Investors can harness
Malaysia's well-established credentials for halal food
production to break into this market segment. Not
surprisingly, equipment and machinery manufacturers
and suppliers are also in demand to support the growth.
Foreign companies interested to fill any of these gaps in
Malaysia will also benefit from being at the source of the
stable agricultural and livestock production.

Contacts
Ministry of Agriculture and Agro-Based Industry
Website: www.moa.gov.my

Malaysian Agricultural Research & Development
Institute (MARDI)
Website: www.mardi.my

Federal Agricultural Marketing Authority (FAMA)
Website: www.famaxchange.org

Malaysian Cocoa Board
Website: www.koko.gov.my

Malaysian Pepper Board
Website: www.mpb.gov.my

Malaysian Pineapple Industry Board
Website: www.mpib.gov.my

Resource-based products

Malaysia is a resource-rich country and a glance out of a plane flying overhead will show either fields of oil palm, rubber trees or vast expanse of rainforest. This in turn supports a range of industries producing wood-based products, rubber products and basic metal products.

Wood

The wood-based industry in Malaysia comprises four major sub-sectors:

- Sawn timber
- Veneer and panel products that include plywood and other reconstituted panel products such as particleboard/chipboard/fibreboard
- Mouldings and builders' joinery and carpentry (BJC) such as doors/windows and their components, panels and flooring board/parquet
- Furniture and furniture components

Rubber-based products

Rubber has been grown in Malaysia as early as the 1890s, when the British brought it over from Brazil. In 2007, the Malaysian rubber products industry employed more than 68,700 workers and contributed RM10.58 billion to the country's export earnings. Rubber products accounted for 1.7% of Malaysia's total exports and 2.3% of Malaysian exports from the manufacturing sector. It is made up of more than 510 manufacturers producing:

- Latex products such as medical, household and industrial gloves, catheters, latex threads, balloons, finger stalls and foam products
- Tyres and tyre-related products

- Industrial rubber products for the automotive, electrical and electronics, machinery and equipment and construction industries

Basic metal products

Malaysia's basic metal industries can be divided primarily into the iron and steel industries and the non-ferrous metal industries. The iron and steel products produced in Malaysia include primary steel products like direct reduced iron, hot briquetted iron, blooms/slabs and steel billets. They also include a wide range of down stream flat and long products like hot-rolled, cold and coated steel coils, roofing sheets, steel pipes and sections, steel billets, steel bars, wire rods, wire mesh, hard drawn wires, galvanised wires, steel wire ropes, steel wire products, stainless steel pipes/pipes fittings and stainless steel wire and fasteners.

The non-ferrous metal segment in Malaysia consists of tin, copper, zinc, lead and aluminium products. Aluminium, the largest sector, produces aluminium sheets/foils, aluminium finstock, aluminium ingots (recycled), aluminium rods and aluminium extruded profiles. The copper sector produces copper rods/wires, copper strips, copper tubes/extrusions and tin metal.

Metals are also mined as raw materials to support the construction industry, electrical/electronic industry, automotive industry, food and packaging industry.

The challenge for the government is to continue to promote and diversify the development of Malaysia's resource-based industries. As resources get scarce, there is an increasing need to find better processes and to ensure better yield. This industry is looking towards life sciences and biotechnology for answers and newer ways of production. Companies are encouraged under the Pioneer Status or Investment Tax Allowance schemes to explore potentials in these areas.

Contacts

The Malaysian Timber Council (MTC)
Website: www.mtc.com.my

6

The Malaysian Timber Industry Board (MTIB)
Website: www.mtib.gov.my

Malaysian Furniture Industry Council (MFIC)
Website: www.mfic.org.my

Malaysian Wood Moulding and Joinery Council
Website: www.mwmjc.com.my

National Timber Certification Council Malaysia
Website: www.mtcc.com.my

Malaysian Rubber Export Promotion Council
Website: www.mrepc.com

Malaysian Rubber Board
Website: www.lgm.gov.my

Malaysian Rubber Products Manufacturers' Association
(MRPMA)
Website: www.mrpma.com

Malaysian Automotive Tyre Manufacturers Industry
Group
Website: www.fmm.org.my

The Malaysian Iron and Steel Industry Federation
Website: www.misif.org.my

Textiles and Apparel

Textiles and apparel manufacturing in Malaysia boomed
in the 1970s and grew to become a major component of
the country's total export earnings. The export value was
RM 10.3 billion in 2007, the ninth largest contributor to
total earnings from manufactured exports. There are 637
licensed companies in production with investments of
RM7.9 billion. The industry employs more than 67,000
workers.

The industry currently encompasses a broad range of
integrated activities ranging from polymerisation and
man-made fibre production, spinning, texturising,
weaving, knitting, dyeing, printing and finishing of yarn
and fabrics to manufacture of clothing and other textile

goods such as carpets, bed and table linen and ropes. Most of these are contract manufacturers for global brand names that value not just low-cost production but have chosen Malaysia for its adherence to fair trade and labour laws. The industry also covers the manufacture of non-woven fabrics for personal care products, made-up garments, furniture and bedding as well as construction and engineering applications.

Notable areas for growth in the textile and apparel industry are:

6

- Creation of local brands, identifying and enabling local designers to enter the international fashion arena. This is not as far-fetched as one thinks. Take Dato Jimmy Choo, OBE for example, he is a London-based luxury fashion designer best known for his hand-made women's shoes, Jimmy Choo Ltd. He was born in Penang, Malaysia and became famous when his shoe designs became the favourite of the late Diana, Princess of Wales. There have been other fashion runway successes and from Malaysia such as Zang Toi and Melinda Looi
- Increase in automation and computerisation of manufacturing processes in many of the small and medium operations to improve output
- Development of new methods and products in dyeing, printing and finishing
- Research and development of new fibres, yarns, industrial and home textiles
- Development of an efficient global distribution and marketing network, and strengthening existing network

To encourage investments in the textiles and apparel industry, several textile products/activities have been gazetted as promoted products/activities under the Promotion of Investment Act 1986 and could be considered for tax incentives in the form of Pioneer Status or Investment Tax Allowance. Interested parties should refer to the MIDA's website for the List of Promoted Activities and Products.

Contacts
Malaysian Textiles Manufacturers
Website: www.fashion-asia.com

Malaysian Knitting Manufacturers Association
Website: www.mkma.org

Service industry
Tourism
The tourism industry contributes an estimated RM 88.9 billion or 13.2% to Malaysia's GDP, providing 1,257,000 jobs (11.6% of total employment) in 2008. What is astonishing is that it is still slated to grow, creating opportunities in this sector. Real GDP growth for tourism industry in Malaysia is expected to be 5.2% in 2008 and to maintain an average growth of 5.3% per annum over the coming ten years.

The string of awards and accolades awarded to Malaysia bears testimony to this fact:

- Malaysia was voted as one of the top five most popular outbound destinations in 2006 out of 100 countries in a poll organised by *Guangzhou Daily*, the biggest South China newspaper which has a daily circulation of 1.8 million
- Malaysia received two awards at the tourism film competition Das Goldene Stadttor (The Golden City Gate) during the world's largest tourism exhibition, ITB, in March 2007. The tropical nature paradise won the gold award for the 'Malaysia Now' global online campaign and a silver award for its 60-second TV commercial themed "The Time is Now, The Place is Malaysia"
- Malaysia was also named the "Best Tourism Destination 2006" by the American business travel magazine *Global Traveller* in the beginning of the year. In early May 2007, *Asfaar Magazine* named Malaysia as the "Best Summer Destination" for United Arab Emirates residents.

Much of the success can be attributed to the government agency in charge of promoting tourism in Malaysia – the Malaysia Tourism Promotion Board (also known as Tourism Malaysia). Tourism Malaysia aims to encourage tourism and its related industries in Malaysia, thus promoting new investments in the country, as well as providing increased employment opportunities. Even if you are not involved in the travel industry, you can still make use of the many attractive programmes to hold your next meeting, incentive trip, convention or exhibition (MICE) activities in Malaysia. Visit the Tourism Malaysia website for more information (www.tourism.gov.my)

6

Education

The government aims to make Malaysia a regional and international centre of education excellence by ensuring that the higher education institutions offer quality education. The Malaysian government's commitment to education is reflected in Malaysia's 2008 Budget – RM12 billion has been allocated for the implementation of various higher education projects and programmes. Of these, overseas education programmes taught partly in Malaysia, with numbers of students on twinning/international joint programmes, are proving to be immensely popular.

As of end 2007, there are 20 public universities and 524 private colleges and institutes of higher education in Malaysia. During this period, there were 46,530 international students from 150 countries studying in Malaysia, of which 12,926 are studying at public universities and 33,604 students at private colleges and institutes of higher learning. Students are predominantly from countries such as Indonesia, China, Iran, Nigeria, Bangladesh, Yemen and Botswana.

The education industry in Malaysia continues to grow rapidly. Countries such as Australia, USA, New Zealand and Canada are making their presence felt in the market here. Germany, Japan, China, Taiwan and France are increasing their marketing activities and are trying to break into the market.

Opportunities for the educational industry include:

- Postgraduate studies, particularly in science, technology, communications and engineering, to meet the accelerated industrial development needs of Malaysia
- Twinning programmes and franchising of degrees
- Joint research, project management and consultancy services including the establishment of education and training institutions
- Distance learning programmes
- Development of curriculum and facilities for technical and vocational education to make training more responsive to industry needs
- "Train the trainer" programmes to increase the number and quality of trainers and instructors

6

Healthcare

The healthcare sector in Malaysia saw more than 341,288 foreigners visiting Malaysia to seek medical treatment under the medical tourism scheme in 2007, an increase of 15%. Foreigners that sought treatment in Malaysian private hospitals include patients from Indonesia, Japan, Europe, India, China, USA, Australia, Singapore and Korea. The Malaysian medical expertise is known to rank among the best in the world and this means that the sector is likely to continue its growth patterns.

There are two types of medical services in Malaysia, namely, the public medical sector and the private medical sector. Private hospitals offer a wide range of health care services and facilities ranging from medical screening to state-of-the-art services at a reasonable cost compared to services of similar standard in other countries.

Malaysian health-care service providers are capable of providing elective and curative procedures in such fields as cardiothoracic treatment and surgery, orthopaedics, obstetrics and gynaecology, ophthalmology, plastic and cosmetic surgery, diagnostic treatment and fertility treatment.

Opportunities in this market include:

- Planning, design, and management of specialised health-care facilities
- Training and specialised medical education for health care personnel (nursing, paramedical, and management programmes)
- Innovative / specialised / niche medical equipment
- Health IT systems and services
- Health consulting services
- Rehabilitation and care facilities for the elderly to cater for the ageing population

6

Contacts

Malaysia Tourism Promotion Board
Website: www.tourism.gov.my

Department of Private Education, Ministry of Education
Website: www.moe.gov.my

Malaysian Association of Private Colleges
Website: www.mapcu.com.my

Association of Private Hospitals of Malaysia
Website : www.hospitals-malaysia.org

Malaysia Medical Association
Website: www.mma.org.my

Information and communications technology

Malaysia has had significant progress in fostering the development of its communications and multimedia industry during the last decade. The government aims to develope Malaysia as a regional services hub and is committed to injecting more spending into this sector. The value of the domestic IT market was RM13 billion in 2007. IT services spending, excluding telecommunications-related spending, is forecast to pass RM3 billion in 2008.

6

The Malaysian Government's Multimedia Super Corridor (MSC) was launched in 1996 to propel the country into the Information Age through a series of specific initiatives. The MSC is a 15km by 50km zone spreading south of Kuala Lumpur. Putrajaya and Cyberjaya, the seats of electronic government and IT city respectively, are located in the centre of the MSC. Developers or heavy users of multimedia or information technology products and services satisfying certain criteria can qualify for MSC Status.

To ensure that the MSC achieves its objectives, the Multimedia Development Corporation (MDC) was established as a 'one-stop super shop' with functions including permit and licensing approvals for companies setting up operations in the MSC.

Companies with approved MSC status will enjoy full tax exemption of their profits for a period of five to ten years, subject to the level of technology transfer. Alternatively, these companies may be granted investment tax allowance (ITA) of 100% on new investments made in the MSC designated cybercities.

Contacts
MSC Malaysia
Website: www.mscmalaysia.my

doing business
in Malaysia

7

doing business in Malaysia

The aim of this section is to
provide a sweeping overview
for the visitor who is considering
the possibility of a local office.
Here are some of the pitfalls and
benefits, an insight into the legal
situation, and some of the major
issues to be considered, such as
recruiting, finding premises, etc.

Considering the sheer amount of incentives available to foreign investors in Malaysia, it makes a lot of sense to at least explore the opportunities in the industry that concerns a business traveller. The cost of doing business is still comparatively low and, combined with a high quality of life and a stable political and social environment, certainly makes a convincing case for Malaysia.

In recent years, foreign equity restrictions have been relaxed, allowing foreign investors in the manufacturing sector to hold 100% equity positions irrespective of their level of exports (with a few exceptions in areas where Malaysia has established capabilities). Only operations with more than RM 2.5 million in paid-up capital or 75 workers or more must apply for a manufacturing licence. Investment incentives include a major reduction in corporate income tax for five years (0-8% versus the normal rate of 28%) for "pioneer status" companies, investment tax allowances and export inducements.

One of the first stops for a feasibility study should be the Malaysian Industrial Development Authority (MIDA) website. There you can access information on topics such as "Cost of Doing Business", "Incentives for Investments", "List of Promoted Activities & Products" and "Guidelines on Expatriate Employment".

MIDA

In 2007, after the less than stellar ranking in the World Bank's survey of 178 countries in all aspects of doing business, Malaysia promptly set up a special task-force to facilitate businesses called PEMUDAH, which means "simplifier" in Malay. In just less than two years, the government succeeded in improving Malaysia's ranking in the latest 2009 survey, jumping five ranks to 20th in overall ease of doing business. While there have been some serious improvements in areas such as getting credit, dealing with construction permits, tax payment and enforcing contracts, starting up business in Malaysia can still be a case of bureaucratic gymnastics. Here are some general guidelines and things to note; for more complete information, including much of the legal fine print, please refer to the respective agencies and ministries involved.

PEMUDAH

7

Setting up a permanent operation

There are two main ways to set up a permanent operation in Malaysia – either by incorporating a local company or by registering as a foreign company with the Companies Commission of Malaysia (SSM). Under the regulations of the Companies Commission of Malaysia, there are different procedures for local companies and foreign companies. While foreign representatives can undertake the procedures described below, it is advisable to find a registered Company Secretary in Malaysia and let local specialists take care of everything. With the right agent, the registration takes just three days and cost just under US$1,000 for a company with less than RM100,000 nominal share capital.

7

Incorporating a local company

The Companies Act 1965 governs all companies in Malaysia. The Act stipulates that a company must be registered with the SSM in order to engage in any business activity. The most common company structure in Malaysia is a company limited by shares. Such limited companies may be either private (Sendirian Berhad or Sdn Bhd) or public (Berhad or Bhd) companies.

To incorporate a local company, one must make an application to the Companies Commission (SSM) to inquire if the intended name is still available for registration. This is done by filling up a prescribed form (Form 13A) and paying the relevant fee (RM30 for each name applied). The procedure usually takes a day.

A reservation period of three months will be granted if the name is available, during which time the company must first get relevant documents such as Memorandum and Articles of Association stamped at the Inland Revenue Board's Stamp Office. This usually takes a day to complete and costs RM100. After which, the original stamped copies of documents such as Memorandum and Articles of Association, Statutory Declaration of Compliance and Statutory Declaration, the letter stating the name approval, valid forms of identification of each director and company secretary, plus relevant fees must be submitted to register with the Companies Commission of Malaysia (SSM). Registration fee is subject to the authorised share capital of the company, RM1,000 for capital up to RM100,000, RM3,000 for capital of RM100,001 – 500,000 and so on.

Locally incorporated companies are required to:

* maintain a registered office in Malaysia where all books and documents required under the provisions of the Act are kept. The name of the company shall appear in legible romanised letters, together with the company number and its seal and documents
* not to deal with its own shares or hold shares in its holding company. Each equity share of a public company carries only one vote at a poll at any general meeting of the company. A private company may, however, provide for varying voting rights for its shareholders
* to employ a company secretary who must be above 18 years of age, a Malaysian or Permanent Resident and who is a member of a prescribed body or is licensed by the Registrar of Companies
* to appoint an approved company auditor to be the company auditor in Malaysia
* to have at least two directors who each has his principal or only place of residence within Malaysia. Directors of public companies or subsidiaries of public companies normally must not exceed 70 years of age. It is not incumbent that a company director also be a shareholder.

The Registrar of Companies will issue a certificate of incorporation once registration procedures are completed and approved.

Registering a foreign company

To register a foreign company in Malaysia, the company must also undergo the same procedure as though incorporating a local company, which is to first file an application to inquire if the intended name is still available. The name to be used to register the foreign company should be the same as that registered in its country of origin.

A reservation period of three months will also be granted if the name is available, during which time the company must submit the following documents to SSM for registration:

1. A certified copy of the certificate of incorporation or registration of the foreign company
2. A certified copy of the foreign company's charter, statute or Memorandum and Articles of Association or other instrument defining its constitution
3. Form 79 (Return By Foreign Company Giving Particulars Of Directors and Changes Of Particulars)
   NOTE: If the list includes directors residing in Malaysia who are members of the local board of directors of the foreign company, a memorandum stating their powers must be executed by or on behalf of the foreign company and submitted to SSM
4. A memorandum of appointment or power of attorney authorising the person(s) residing in Malaysia to accept on behalf of the foreign company any notices required to be served on such foreign company
5. Form 80 (Statutory Declaration By Agent Of Foreign Company)
6. Additional documents consisting of:
   The original Form 13A
   A copy of the letter from SSM approving the name of the foreign company.

Documents in any language other than Bahasa Malaysia or English must have an accompanying certified translation. The relevant fee that is based on the nominal share capital of the foreign company is also payable upon submission of the registration. In determining the registration fees, the nominal share capital of the foreign company should first be converted to the Malaysian currency (Ringgit Malaysia) at the prevailing exchange rate. In the event a foreign company does not offer any share capital, a flat rate of RM 1,000 shall be paid to SSM.

The Companies Commission will issue the company
a certificate of registration upon compliance with the
registration procedures and submission of duly
completed registration documents.

Representative or regional office

However, if you are considering an intermediate
solution, you can also look into a third option,
which is to set up a representative or regional office.
Representative and regional offices are not allowed to
carry out any business transaction or derive income from
their operations. They should be totally funded from
sources outside Malaysia and are, therefore, not required
to be incorporated or registered under the Companies
Act 1965. However, it allows a foreign company to have
a legal entity in Malaysia and obtain
a work permit for its representative(s) without having
paid-up capital or paying corporate tax in Malaysia.
Expatriates working in regional offices are taxed only
on the portion of their chargeable income attributable
to the number of days that they are in Malaysia.

The setting-up of these offices and the application of
work permits for the representative and his dependants
all have to be approved by the Malaysian Industrial
Development Authority (MIDA). The approval is granted
for two years and can be renewed for up to ten years.

For more information, visit the Malaysian Industrial
Development Authority (www.mida.gov.my) or the
Malaysian Companies Commission (www.ssm.com.my)
websites. For information on company secretarial
services in Malaysia, see The Malaysian Institute of
Chartered Secretaries and Administrators
(www.maicsa.or.my).

Setting up an office

Rental rates for prime office space differs depending on
the state. As a guideline, gross rental per square metre
per month is between RM15 and around RM35 for
most states with the exception of Kuala Lumpur and
the surrounding Klang Valley. There, rental rates are
between RM30 and RM165.

7

You can also look into cost-effective virtual office services that offer not just a business address and mail-forwarding but also a receptionist. These services are usually based on a yearly fee (usage of business address and mail-forwarding) or a monthly fee with receptionist service.

Financial reporting

The Companies Act 1965 requires that a corporation should prepare annual accounts and have it audited before tabling it at an annual general meeting of members for their approval at least once in each calendar year. The accounts should be prepared in accordance with the Companies Act 1965 which includes compliance with approved accounting standards. Accounts have also to be prepared for the Inland Revenue Board for the purpose of assessment for income tax.

The Inland Revenue Board of Malaysia
Website: www.hasil.org.my

Accounting and auditing

Malaysia uses International Accounting Standards and International Standards on Auditing as a basis for the setting of approved accounting standards and approved standards on auditing respectively.

Taxation

The taxation rates and laws in Malaysia are designed to attract foreign investors into Malaysia and are therefore much lower and more liberal than in most industrialised countries. For instance, while all income accrued in or derived from Malaysia is subject to income tax, income received in Malaysia derived from sources outside Malaysia by any person or company (remitted from overseas) is, in most cases, exempted from tax.

Malaysia has also signed Tax Treaties with 59 countries to avoid double taxation on cross-border flows of income and to provide tax credits or exemptions, thus eliminating double taxation. For the full list of these countries see MIDA's website for 'Taxation'.

Company tax

A company, whether resident or not, is assessable on income accrued in or derived from Malaysia. Income derived from sources outside Malaysia and remitted by a resident company is exempted from tax, except in the case of the banking and insurance business, and sea and air transport undertakings. A company is considered a resident in Malaysia if the control and management of its affairs are exercised in Malaysia.

Effective from the year assessment of 2007, the corporate tax rate is reduced to 27%. The tax rate is to be further reduced to 26% in 2008 and to 25% in 2009.

A company carrying on petroleum upstream operations is subject to a Petroleum Income Tax of 38%.

7

Income tax

All residents (local or foreign) are liable to tax on income accrued in or derived from Malaysia. Effective from the year assessment 2004, income remitted to Malaysia by a resident individual is exempted from tax. A resident individual is taxed on his chargeable income after deducting personal relief at a graduated rate from 0% to a maximum of 28%.

A non-resident individual will be taxed only on income earned in Malaysia. The rate of tax depends on the individual's resident status, which is determined by the duration of his stay in the country. Generally, an individual who is in Malaysia for at least 182 days in a calendar year is regarded as a tax resident. A non-resident individual is liable to tax at the rate of 28% without any personal relief. However, he can claim rebates in respect of fees paid to the government for the issuance of an employment work permit.

Sales and service tax

Sales tax is a single-stage tax imposed at the import or manufacturing levels. In Malaysia, it is generally from 5% to 10%. Certain non-essential foodstuffs and building materials are taxed at 5%, general goods at 10%, liquor at 20% and cigarettes at 25%. Companies with a sales turnover of less than RM100,000 and companies with Licensed Manufacturing

7

Warehouse(LMW) status are exempted from this licensing requirement. However, companies with a sales turnover of less than RM100,000 have to apply for a certificate of exemption from licensing.

A 5% service tax applies to certain prescribed goods and services in Malaysia including food, drinks and tobacco; provision of rooms for lodging and premises for meetings, conventions, and cultural and fashion shows; health services, and provision of accommodation and food by private hospitals.

Excise duty

Excise duties are levied on selected products manufactured in Malaysia, namely; cigarettes, tobacco products, alcoholic beverages, playing cards, mah-jong tiles and motor vehicles.

Others

There is no Real Property Gains Tax as of 1 April 2007. Over the last few years, Malaysia also has begun to abolish import duties on a wide range of raw materials, components and machinery. Furthermore, Malaysia is committed to the ASEAN Common Effective Preferential Tariffs (CEPT) scheme under which all industrial goods traded within ASEAN have import duties imposed of 0% to 5%. The customs tariff regime in Malaysia is based on the Harmonized Commodity Description and Coding System of goods classification.

Contacts

Inland Revenue Board of Malaysia – www.hasil.org.my
Royal Malaysian Customs – www.customs.gov.my

Manpower and employment

One of Malaysia's key assets is the vibrant and educated labour force. Most Malaysian youths who enter the labour market will have undergone at least eleven years of school education, that is, up to secondary school level. They are, therefore, easy to train in new techniques and skills. There is an increasing supply of professionals, technologists and skilled workers graduating from both local and foreign universities, colleges and technical and industrial training institutions. Labour costs in Malaysia are low in comparison with the industrialised countries while labour productivity remains high.

Wages

There is no national minimum wage law applicable to the manufacturing sector in Malaysia. Basic wage rates vary according to location and industrial sector. There are, however, minimum conditions for employment.

Supplementary benefits include a bonus, free uniforms, free or subsidised transport, performance incentives. Other benefits vary from company to company.

For details on salaries and benefits for the manufacturing sector, please refer to MIDA's brochure 'The Costs of Doing Business in Malaysia'.

7

Statutory contributions
Employees Provident Fund

When employing in Malaysia, employers need to be aware of the strictly enforced Employees Provident Fund (EPF or Kumpulan Wang Simpanan Pekerja). This is a mandatory social security or retirement planning savings fund for all employed Malaysian Citizens or Permanent Residents. The fund is accrued monthly into a member's account, which is maintained and invested by the government agency.

EPF functions by procuring at least 11% of each member's monthly salary and storing it in a savings account, while the member's employer is obligated to additionally fund at least 12% of the employee's salary to the savings fund at the same time. The fund can only be withdrawn when members are 50 years old, during which they may withdraw only 30% of their EPF; members who are 55 years old or older may withdraw all of their EPF.

All foreign workers earning less than RM2,500 per month are required to contribute 11% of their monthly wages while the employers are required to contribute RM5 per employee per month.

Self-employed persons, expatriates (with monthly wages of RM2,500 and above) and domestic helpers that is, persons who are employed to work in or connected with work in a private dwelling house, including valets and gardeners, and who are paid from the private account of the employer are exempted from compulsory contributions. They can, however, choose to contribute to the Fund.

All employers must register their employees with the EPF within seven days of employment.

Employment Provident Fund – www.kwsp.gov.my

Employee's social security

The Social Security Organisation (SOCSO) administers two social security schemes to protect workers earning wages not exceeding RM3,000 per month. The two social security schemes are: Employment Injury Insurance Scheme and Invalidity Pension Scheme.

SOCSO

The Employment Injury Insurance Scheme provides employees with coverage by way of cash benefits and medical care in the event of any disablement or death due to employment injury. The contribution is borne solely by the employer and is about 1.25% of the wages of an employee.

The Invalidity Pension Scheme provides 24-hour coverage to employees against invalidity or death due to any cause not connected with his employment. However, the employee must fulfil the condition to be eligible for invalidity pension. A contribution under this scheme is 1% of the employee's wages and is to be shared equally by the employer and employee.

Any employer who hires one or more employees as defined under the Act is required to register and make contributions to SOCSO.

Social Security Organisation – www.perkeso.gov.my

Employment of Foreign Workers

In Malaysia, foreign workers can be employed in the manufacturing, construction, services (domestic servants, restaurant workers, cleaners, workers in cargo handling, workers in welfare homes, launderettes, island resorts and caddies in golf clubs) and agricultural sectors. All applications from companies located in Peninsular Malaysia should be submitted to the Ministry of Home Affairs. Employment of foreign workers must conform to the approved nationalities set out in specific industries.

All applications from companies located in Peninsular Malaysia should be submitted to the Ministry of Home Affairs. Applications to employ foreign workers will only be considered when efforts to find qualified local citizens and permanent residents have failed.

An annual levy on foreign workers is imposed as follows:

7

Approved Sectors	Annual Levy
Manufacturing	RM1,200
Services	RM1,200-1,800
Construction	RM1,200
Agricultural	RM 360-540
Domestic Help	RM 360

For further information, please visit the Malaysia's Immigration Department Website at www.imi.gov.my

Infrastructure incentives

Industrial Estates, Free Trade Zones and Licensed Manufacturing Warehouses have been established throughout the country to cater specifically to the needs of manufacturing companies and encourage export-oriented production.

Malaysia has over 200 industrial estates or parks developed by government agencies, namely, the State Economic Development Corporations (SEDCs), Regional Development Authorities (RDAs), port authorities and municipalities. Industrial estates provide basic infrastructure such as roads, water, power and telecommunications facilities.

7

As their name implies, Free Trade Zones are specifically designed for the manufacture or assembling of products essentially for export. Imports of raw materials, parts, machinery and equipment for export manufacture are subject to minimum customs control and formalities as are the exports of Free Trade Zones. To date, 18 Free Zones have been established.

Licensed Manufacturing Warehouses have been established where a Free Trade Zone is neither practical nor desirable and are accorded similar facilities.

Special provisions and incentives also exist to encourage foreign companies to establish operations in the Multimedia Super Corridor. Companies granted the MSC Status enjoy a set of incentives and benefits such as a five-year tax exemption, ten-year capital tax allowance and research and development grants.

Preference is given to foreign investments and joint ventures with the greatest potential for technology and knowledge transfer. Applications for MSC Status should be submitted to MSC Malaysia (www.mscmalaysia.my).

Intellectual Property Laws

WIPO

Intellectual property protection in Malaysia comprises patents, trade-marks, industrial designs, copyrights, geographical indications and layout designs of integrated circuits. Malaysia is a member of the World Intellectual Property Organization (WIPO) and a signatory to the Paris Convention and Berne Convention that govern these intellectual property rights.

In addition, Malaysia is also a signatory to the Agreement on Trade Related Aspects of Intellectual Property Rights (TRIPS) signed under the auspices of the World Trade Organization (WTO). Therefore, Malaysia's intellectual property laws conform with international standards and provide adequate protection for both local and foreign investors.

Patents registered in Malaysia generally have a 15-year duration, which can be extended under certain circumstances. Processing time for trade mark registration may be long and drawn-out but measures are put in place to smooth out the processes. Copyright protection extends to computer software and lasts for 50 years. The Copyright Act includes enforcement provisions allowing government officials to enter and search premises suspected of infringement and to make arrests, seize infringing copies and reproduction equipment.

However, piracy rates for software, music and video disks are still high in Malaysia despite the government's efforts. Pirated products believed to have originated in Malaysia have been identified throughout the Asia Pacific region. Malaysia continues to initiate a high-profile campaign against piracy of software and movies throughout the country. Cyberlaw legislation was enacted to assist in the development of the Multimedia Super Corridor, but enforcement has been sporadic at best.

For more information, see:

The Ministry of Domestic Trade and Consumer Affairs
Website: www.kpdnhep.gov.my

Intellectual Property Corporation of Malaysia
Website: www.myipo.gov.my

7

Kuala Lumpur

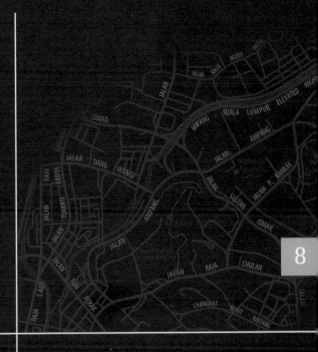

8

Kuala Lumpur and the Klang Valley

Kuala Lumpur and the Klang Valley

The nation's capital

History

Standing in the middle of the modern, bustling Kuala Lumpur today, it is hard to think that all that came about from so little and in such a short span of time. Kuala Lumpur began life as a collection of shacks built by the Chinese miners at the junction of Kelang and Gombak rivers, believed to be in 1857. They were attracted to this inhospitable area by the lure of massive tin deposits. The name they gave this new settlement – which translates as 'muddy confluence' – is hardly a propitious one. In fact, its early history was one plagued with disasters such as floods, fires, disease and the civil wars associated with frontier towns.

Kuala Lumpur did not gain its urban status until the end of the 19th century, when it was chosen to be the capital of the Federated Malay States by the then colonial masters, the British, in 1896.

8

With the new capital status came growth and development. In response to a major fire that destroyed the town's structures, the British Resident of Selangor mandated that all buildings be constructed out of brick and tile. Consequently, many of the new brick buildings began to mirror distinctive shophouse architecture in southern China, with 'five-foot-ways' and ornate displays of skilled Chinese carpentry. Meanwhile, British subjects who have spent time in India and other Far East colonies decided that the standard European architecture for its administrative buildings would not be appropriate for an Asian capital and proposed a fusion of styles with Moghul/Mughal influences in its place.

Kuala Lumpur continued to grow despite two world wars, the rubber and tin commodity crash and The State Of Emergency (1948-60) during which Malaya was preoccupied with the communist insurgency. In 1957, the Federation of Malaya gained its independence from British rule. An event commemorated each year on 31st August with shouts of "Merdeka!", a Malay word meaning independence and a lavish parade on Merdeka Square. Kuala Lumpur remained the capital through the formation of Malaysia, achieving city status in 1972, and was established as the Federal Territory in 1974.

8

Kuala Lumpur today

The city today is a dynamic metropolis that is home
to 1.8 million people. Greater Kuala Lumpur, known
as Klang Valley, supports more than seven million
people. It is the fastest growing urban area, in terms of
both population and economy. It is the largest city in
Malaysia and is also the seat of the Parliament of
Malaysia and the legislative centre.

Remnants of the past are still very much a part of Kuala
Lumpur and that is what gives this bustling city its
charm. Visitors can revel in some of the finest examples
of colonial structures in the old administrative quarters
clustered around Merdeka Square. Many of the old "five-
foot way" shophouses have been refurbished and some
even revived as small business shop fronts or have been
turned into various entertainment venues such as cafes,
restaurants, clubs and bars. The area around Merdeka
Square, Sultan Abdul Samad Building, Selangor Club
and what is now known as Chinatown, forms the
City Centre.

But the most striking symbol of modern Kuala Lumpur
is surely the Petronas Twin Towers. This architectural
masterpiece of glass and steel is so many things to so
many people. Once a holder of the title 'tallest building
of the world' until it was overtaken by Taipei's 101, it is
a sumbol of Malaysia's booming 1990s economy. Today
it is still the headquarter of Malaysia's most important
company, PETRONAS, and is the most photographed
landmark of Malaysia, a legacy of Tun Dr Mahathir's
reign as prime minister and the pride of a new generation
of Malaysians who are confident about Malaysia's future.
The list goes on.

Opened in 1999, each of the Petronas' Twin Towers
stands at 88-storeys, rising 452 metres high into KL's (as
the locals refer to Kuala Lumpur) skyline. The towers still
reign as the world's tallest twin towers and for housing
the tallest sky bridge in the world. It is the epicentre of
the city's 'Golden Triangle', bounded by Jalan Ampang,
Jalan Tun Razak, and Jalan Imbi.

The Golden Triangle region, located to the north-east
of the City Centre, embraces the throbbing night-life of

Jalan P. Ramlee, the forever-teeming shopping district of Bukit Bintang, the five-star hotel strip of Jalan Sultan Ismail, the gleaming office skyscrapers on Jalan Raja Chulan and last, but not least, the sprawling vicinity of Petronas Towers, known as Kuala Lumpur City Centre (KLCC).

Outside the city centre, **Bangsar** is one of the most popular local nightspots. The two main streets leading into Bangsar, Telawi and Maarof, are lined with bars, clubs, pubs and bistros. It offers a wide variety of dining options, from delectable street food to up-market eateries that are among the finest in the country. Needless to say, the surrounding residential area is a favourite among expatriates and affluent Malaysians who add to the vibrant clientele.

Kuala Lumpur is no stranger to the notion of urban sprawl. It forms part of a conurbation together with the adjoining districts of Selangor state, collectively known as the **Klang Valley**. Originally a satellite town to accommodate the working population of KL, **Petaling Jaya** (known as PJ) is mostly a place for locals, with few tourist attractions. However, there are quite a number of major multinational companies based in the area. So there may be a chance that a business traveller might spend nights here instead of in the congested city centre.

Another major town of the Klang Valley is **Subang Jaya**, which is also known as an educational hub for its many educational institutions in and around the area. **Shah Alam** and **Port Klang** are the major industrialised towns within the Klang Valley.

Kuala Lumpur holds the dubious distinction of having the cheapest five-star hotels in the world, much to the delight of many travellers. Here are some of the recommended hotels and dining options, according to the various districts outlined above:

Please note that rates quoted below are indicative and are subject to change

8

Golden Triangle Hotels

Mandarin Oriental Kuala Lumpur gets top marks for the perfect place to stay, whether for business or pleasure. Located directly adjacent to the Petronas Twin Towers, the luxury hotel is also in front of the tranquil KLCC park that stretches 50 acres. The hotel chain is internationally renowned for its discreet and attentive service. The lush furnishings and luxurious amenities are all carefully selected to ease the stress of travel away. The only slight drawback is that the hotel has aged, albeit elegantly, and is being glossed over in favour of the newer kids on the block. The hotel boasts one of the best Chinese restaurants in Kuala Lumpur – Lai Po Heen. It serves innovative Chinese delicacies and dim sum and is fully halal, making it a discerning choice to host your local Muslim counterparts.

8

Mandarin Oriental Kuala Lumpur
Kuala Lumpur City Centre
Kuala Lumpur 50088
Malaysia
Tel: +60 (3) 2179 8818
Fax: +60 (3) 2179 8659
Website: www.mandarinoriental.com
Rates from RM499 per night

Hotel Maya is the newest hot property in KL's competitive hotel scene that is located in the vicinity of KLCC. Rising above the deluge of glossy-but-staid five-star hotels, Hotel Maya offers itself as the boutique urban resort. It displays a keen sense of design trend that is characteristic of hip and stylish boutique city hotels. What is different here is that it is all offered up with a distinctive Asian touch. This essential ingredient warms up the clean, minimalist lines and adds dimension to the stay here. The spa and health facilities here are more than noteworthy; remember to treat yourself to that massage before you leave.

Hotel Maya
138 Jalan Ampang
50450 Kuala Lumpur
Malaysia
Tel: +60 (3) 2711 8866
Fax: +60 (3) 2711 9966

Website: www.hotelmaya.com.my
Rates from RM378 per night

Traders Hotel is located just opposite Petronas Twin Towers and is a well-appointed business hotel that more than exceeds its class. Service is impeccable, the rooms are immaculate and the facilities, many of which have stunning views of the city, are outstanding. The buffet breakfast is definitely worth waking up for. What more do you need?

Traders Hotel Kuala Lumpur
Kuala Lumpur City Centre
Kuala Lumpar 50088
Malaysia
Tel: +60 (3) 2332 9888
Fax: +60 (3) 2332 2666
Website: www.shangri-la.com
Rates from RM370 per night

A stay at **The Ritz Carlton Kuala Lumpur** will not break the bank but it might be one of the few times you get treated to the personal butler service that comes with every room. The property is well located in Bukit Bintang, tucked away from the usual heavy pedestrian traffic that plagues the central shopping district. Upscale retail shops and endless dining and entertainment options are available literally outside your doorstep. Luxurious lodgings and unsurpassed convenience is again slightly offset by the dated furnishings.

The Ritz-Carlton Kuala Lumpur
168, Jalan Imbi
Kuala Lumpur 55100
Malaysia
Tel: +60 (3) 2142 8000
Fax: +60 (3) 2143 8080
Website: www.ritzcarlton.com
Rates from RM512 per night

In a similar class to The Ritz, you can also check into the newer **The Westin Kuala Lumpur** or the **JW Marriott Hotel, Kuala Lumpur.** The three properties are located within minutes from one another and all offer the same five-star luxury and elegance.

8

The Westin Kuala Lumpur
199, Jalan Bukit Bintang
Kuala Lumpur 55100
Malaysia
Tel: +60 (3) 2731 8333
Website: www.starwoodhotels.com
Rates from RM449 per night

JW Marriott Hotel Kuala Lumpur
183 Jalan Bukit Bintang
Kuala Lumpur 55100
Malaysia
Tel: +60 (3) 2715 9000
Fax: +60 (3) 2715 7000
Website: www.marriott.com
Rates from RM450 per night

8

In the comfort class, with rates from RM200, you can rely on local establishments like **The Federal Hotel** that has been operating as a business hotel on Bukit Bintang Road for more than 50 years. The hotel has been recently refurbished and remains a favourite for local businessmen. Under the same management group, **Hotel Capitol** offers the business traveller even more choices. Choose between comfortable, value-for-money rooms or contemporary '10rooms' that have been revamped into designer lofts.

The Federal Kuala Lumpur
35 Jalan Bukit Bintang
55100 Kuala Lumpur
Malaysia
Tel: +60 (3) 2148 9166
Fax: +60 (3) 2148 2877
Website: www.federal.com.my
Rates from RM208 per night

Hotel Capitol
Jalan Bulan,
Off Jalan Bukit Bintang
55100 Kuala Lumpur
Malaysia
Tel: +60 (3) 2143 7000
Fax: +60 (3) 2143 0000
Website: www.federal.com.my
Rates from RM185 per night

In the serviced apartments category, Crown Regency Serviced Suites stands out for its value for money and excellent location. On the doorsteps of this hotel is KL's famed nightlife on Jalan P. Ramlee. Ask for higher floor if you do not want to be disturbed. Further along the road is the luxuriously appointed Ascott Kuala Lumpur. This prestigious property offers the very best in service and facilities and is steps away from the Petronas Twin Towers and Suria KLCC shopping centre.

Serviced apartments

Crown Regency Serviced Suites
12 Jalan P. Ramlee
50250 Kuala Lumpur
Malaysia
Tel: +60 (3) 2162 3888
Fax: +60 (3) 2162 1333
Website: www.crownregency.com.my
Rates from RM258 per night

Ascott Kuala Lumpur
No 9 Jalan Pinang
50450 Kuala Lumpur
Malaysia
Tel: +60 (3) 2142 6868
Fax: 60 (3) 2142 9888
Website: www.the-ascott.com
Rates from RM650 per night

8

Dining and Nightlife

The Golden Triangle offers the business traveller the best in terms of dinning options and night entertainment. Around KLCC, you can find fine dining options and large-scale themed clubs like Zouk, Beach Club and Nuovo. Bukit Bintang is a compact strip offering everything from famous street food to high-end French food. The listing below is of just some of the more notable establishments and are chosen with the needs of the business traveller in mind.

Food at **Madam Kwan's** is not to be missed. Located on Level 4, Suria KLCC, Lot 420/421 (Tel: +60 (3) 2026 2297), this modern restaurant allows you to taste local food in comfort. Before you think of it as a sanitised outlet for tourists, it is actually one of the few places that serve up authentic Straits Chinese cuisine. This place is good for a quick business lunch. The signature dishes to try are Nasi Lemak or the Indonesian Nasi Bojari. Both of these are rice dishes that come with accompanying curries and condiments that can be spicy. There is also an outlet in Bangsar that has a more traditional ambience – 65 Telawi 3, Bangsar Baru, 59100 Kuala Lumpur, (Tel: +60 (3) 2284 2297).

Bijan Bar and Restaurant is a beautiful restaurant that serves local Malay specialties. Winner of the best restaurant award from Tourism Malaysia, the food is of a consistently high standard. Located in the heart of the Golden Triangle it is tucked away in a tranquil oasis. The building is a single-storey house with an open terrace, where warm tropical-wood interiors are matched with a modern look. This place is perfect for a long relaxing lunch or an intimate dinner (3 Jalan Ceylon, Tel: 3 2031 3575, www.bijanrestaurant.com).

Shang Palace is located inside the Shangri-La Hotel and is a traditional Chinese restaurant that offers exquisite dim sum. Shang, along with Lai Po Heen (in Mandarin Oriental Hotel, Tel: 3 2179 8885), is hugely popular for business lunches in Kuala Lumpur. (11 Jalan Sultan Ismail, Tel: 3 2074 3904).

Scalini's is a fancy dining outlet located on a hilltop along the Sultan Ismail Road. Expect superb Italian cuisine in a contemporary setting designed by internationally-renowned New York-based architect Tony Chi (19, Jalan Sultan Ismail, Tel: 3 2145 3211).

Asian Heritage Row, located on Jalan Doraisamy, off Jalan Sultan Ismail, is a quaint collection of restaurants, bars and clubs that are all set in beautifully restored 80-year-old pre-war shophouses. Start the evening with dinner and choose from options ranging from Indian to Indochinese then hop on over to any of the other establishments for drinks and cocktails or live music and some clubbing (www.asianheritagerow.com).

Frangipani Restaurant & Bar first opened its doors in 2001 and instantly became the darling of the Kuala Lumpur night scene. It is indisputably one of the coolest

8

venues in town. Comprising two floors, the stunning ground floor is used for dining. The seating area encircles a reflective pool, where diners enjoy contemporary French cuisine. The upper area houses the club and bar where cocktails are served and consumed by beautiful people. (25 Changkat Bukit Bintang, Tel: 3 2144 3001, www.frangipani.com.my).

If European cuisine is not on your travel agenda or if you are dining alone, then head over to **Jalan Alor** for a serious assault on your taste buds and for true local flavour. Here you find an entire street dedicated to hawker stalls that serve up local delights ranging from Chinese, Indian and Malay food. Located right next to Bukit Bintang, Jalan Alor is extremely popular with the locals and with tourists for offering delicious food served in a traditional open-air atmosphere, with chairs and tables on the kerb and roadside. After you have had your fill, there's always room for a nightcap and/or some clubbing. You are only a few streets away from Frangipani (see above) after all.

8

Elsewhere in Kuala Lumpur
Hotels

If effortless accessibility to the Kuala Lumpur International Airport is an imperative for your visit to the city, then **The Hilton Kuala Lumpur** is second to none. Located two minutes from the KL Sentral Station, where high-speed trains whisk you off to KLIA in 30 minutes at a regular interval, you can also access major areas of KL via excellent city rail connections. This supremely comfortable hotel is marvellous for travellers hopping in and out of the city with time restrictions and who have, therefore, little time to be caught in the notorious KL peak-hour traffic.

Hilton Kuala Lumpur Hotel
3 Jalan Stesen Sentral
Kuala Lumpur
Malaysia 50470
Tel: +60 (3) 2264 2264
Fax: +60 (3) 2264 2266
Website: www1.hilton.com
Rates from RM485 per night

Rooms in **Carcosa Seri Negara** are housed in two exquisite mansions built by the first colonial Resident-General in 1904, originally designed to accommodate visiting heads of state. The hotel sits atop a hill, overlooking the city's sedate Lake Gardens, just outside the heart of KL. The place epitomises old-world charm that harks back to the days of colonial Malaya. The elegant thirteen-suite hotel comes with round-the-clock butler service and offers two restaurants, a cocktail bar and a much-raved-about afternoon tea. Perfect for business travellers with a few days to spare in Kuala Lumpur who would like to seek solace in a quiet place not too far away.

Carcosa Seri Negara
Taman Tasik Perdana
Kuala Lumpur 50480
Malaysia
Tel: +60 (3) 2282 1888
Fax: +60 (3) 2282 6868
Website: www.ghmhotels.com
Rates from RM1,100 per night

Dining and nightlife

Tamarind Springs is set on the edge of a forest and serves authentic Indochinese cuisine from Cambodia, Laos and Vietnam. Here, diners can enjoy their meals on open balconies that nestle on treetops, making this a very special place to dine. This delightful restaurant is about a 15-minute drive from KLCC. (Jalan 1, Taman TAR, Ampang, Tel: +60 (3) 4256 9300, www.tamarindrestaurants.com).

Bangsar 'Mamaks' are much-cherished local institutions. They are usually late-opening establishments run by Indian Muslims and serve up delectable dishes like a large variety of *chanai* (*roti prata* to some), *mee goreng* and tandoori. The casual open-concept setting (plastic chairs spill out of the restaurant onto the walkways) provides late-night revellers with much needed suppers or pre-clubbing food. Enjoy a meal in true local style or sip a cup of *teh tarik*, a type of sweet milk tea and a popular remedy for the slightly inebriated Bangsar party animals.

8

After your meal, take in the sights and sounds of the nightlife in Bangsar. Noteworthy venues include old-timers like Telawi Street Bistro and La Bodega, swanky joints like Alexis and The Talk, and down-to-earth bars like The Social and Bar Flam.

(Along and around Telawi Street and Jalan Maarof).

More street food and this time – Chinese street food that can be found, where else but **Chinatown**? Head down to Petaling Street and savour the madness of it all. Stalls line the streets selling everything a tourist can ever wish to buy. But for culinary delights, head to the middle of it all, where **Petaling Street** intersects with **Hang Jebat Road** and there you can find hawker stalls selling all kinds of food. Try the roast duck of legendary fame from Sai Ngan Chai. Order it whole or in part and the vendor will serve it chopped up with a tantalising black sauce. Claypot chicken makes for a great accompanying dish for the duck or you can also try the different types of seafood cooked in blazing woks. *Bak Kut Teh* is another famous dish from this part of the globe. Visitors may be confounded by the hype around this delicately spiced herbal soup cooked with pork spare ribs but it is the sworn favorite of many locals.

Klang Valley
Petaling Jaya

One World Hotel is a new 438-room 5-star hotel located in the heart of Petaling Jaya that adjoins One Utama, one of the best-regarded shopping malls in Kuala Lumpur for its convenience and prestige. The surrounding amenities make your stay in the suburbs a pleasant and practical one.

One World Hotel
First Avenue, Bandar Utama City Centre
47800 Petaling Jaya
Selangor
Malaysia
Tel: +60 (3) 7681 1111 / 7712 2222
Fax: +60 (3) 7681 1188 / 7712 2388
Website: www.oneworldhotel.com.my
Rates from RM400 per night

8

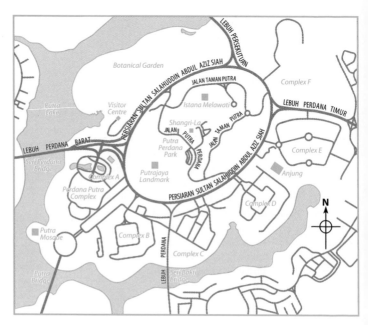

Putrajaya

Putrajaya

Putrajaya Shangri-La Malaysia overlooks gorgeous
fountains and gardens in this new administrative centre.
As always, you can expect the incomparable level of
luxury and service synonymous with the brand.

Putrajaya ShangriFI La Malaysia
Taman Putra Perdana
Presint 1
62000 Wilayah Perseketuan Putrajaya,
Malaysia
Tel: +60 (3) 8887 8888
Fax: +60 (3) 8887 8889
Website: www.shangri-la.com
Rates from RM330 per night

Pullman Putrajaya Lakeside opens in January 2009 and
offers a premier hotel experience for discerning business
travellers.

Pullman Putrajaya Lakeside
Lot 5P2 Precinct 5
Putrajaya 62000
www.pullmanhotels.com
Rates from RM260 per night

Shah Alam

The Club at The Saujana is another property managed
by the same hotel management group as Carcosa Seri
Negara. Opened on 1 September 2008, this is slated to
be the finest and most luxurious boutique resort in the
city. The resort recreates much of the winning formula
of its older sister. It is also nestled amongst lush tropical
gardens, boasts immensely spacious rooms and suites
and will feature the same level of attentive service. The
property is also surrounded by two 18-hole championship
golf courses and is strategically located 30 minutes from
Kuala Lumpur city centre and 35 minutes from the
Kuala Lumpur International Airport in Shah Alam.

The Club at the Saujana
Jalan Lapangan Terbang SAAS
Shah Alam
Selangor Darul Ehsan
Kuala Lumpur 40150
Malaysia
Tel: +60 (3) 7843 1234
Fax: +60 (3) 7846 3008
Website: www.ghmhotels.com
Rates from RM990 per night

Concorde Hotel Shah Alam is your less opulent choice.
A standard business hotel, it offers comfortable rooms,
some of which have views of the enchanting Blue Mosque.

Concorde Hotel Shah Alam
3 Jalan Tengku Ampuan Zabedah C9/C
40100 Shah Alam
Selangor Darul Ehsan
Malaysia
Tel: +60 (3) 5512 2200
Fax: +60 (3) 5512 2233
Website: www.concorde.net
Rates from RM228 per night

8

Subang

Sunway Resort Hotel & Spa is an integrated resort with its own shopping mall, water theme park and full conference facilities. Travellers can choose from a range of accommodations such as standard room, suite, villa or apartment duplex. It is well-located in the education hub, making it easier for business visitors exploring opportunities in the sector.

Sunway Resort Hotel & Spa
Persiaran Lagoon, Bandar Sunway,
46150 Petaling Jaya
Selangor Darul Ehsan
Malaysia
Tel: +60 (3) 7492 8000
Fax: +60 (3) 7492 8001
Website: kualalumpur.sunwayhotels.com
Rates from RM305 per night

8

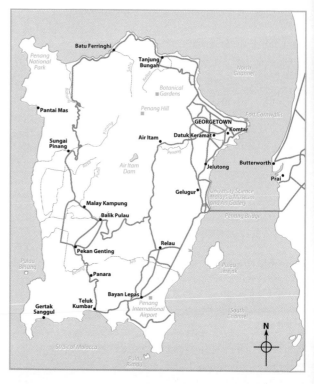

Penang

9

major cities
in Malaysia

major cities
in Malaysia

9

Things to do and see in Malaysia

Peninsular Malaysia

An estimated 80 per cent of Malaysia's total population lives and works in Peninsular Malaysia. Many of the major industries and businesses are also located here. Except for some designated industrial and trading zones, most of the developments are centred in and around the major state capitals.

Penang

Penang is an island state off the northen tip of the Peninsular. Founded in 1786 by Captain Francis Light of the British East India Company, Penang later formed part of the Straits Settlement Agreement between the British and the Dutch. Today, the historic centre and state capital, where ships on the spice trade routes used to dock for refuelling, still retains its original name – Georgetown. Penang is linked to mainland Peninsular Malaysia by Penang Bridge, one Asia's longest bridges. It is also accessible by ferry from Butterworth, and by rail or by air. The Penang International Airport has direct flights from Kuala Lumpur, Singapore, Bangkok, Nagoyra, Medan, Xiamen (China) and Madras.

Penang's maze of narrow streets still features many of the old buildings from the days of the East India Company, offering visitors an insight into bygone days. Its reputation for the best food in Malaysia makes Penang a popular tourist destination for locals and foreigners alike. Just sample some of the local favourites at **Gurney Drive** to find out for yourself. Some important sights include the elaborate Chinese clan houses (**Khoo Kongsi**), the nostalgic **Eastern and Oriental Hotel** and **Cheong Fatt Tze Mansion** that features the best-preserved 19th-century mansion featuring exquisite traditional Chinese carpentry. Visitors are also encouraged to stop by **Penang Hill** to take in a panoramic view of the city or to book a beachfront chalet in **Batu Ferringhi**, the northern coastline which borders Penang.

Penang is one of the most industrialised states in Malaysia and it plays host to a multitude of foreign multinational companies. It has a particularly well-developed information and communications technology industry as well as an electronic and electrical manufacturing sector.

9

Foreign companies such as Intel, Advance Micro Devices and Sony are just some of the key players that have operations in Penang. It attracted RM3.1 billion in foreign investments in 2007 and is likely to match it in 2008.

Sixteen kilometres south of Georgetown lies the town of Bayan Lepas. It is here that you find Penang's Free Industrial Zone, where many of the multinational companies and Penang International airport are located. The 56 hectres enclosed by Penang Port and Butterworth Deep Water Wharves is a gazetted Free Commercial Zone where import and export activities including distribution, trading, consolidation, storage and trans-shipment for most goods, are not subject to customs duty, excise duty, sales tax or service tax.

Contacts
Penang Tourism – www.tourismpenang.gov.my
Penang Development Corporation – www.pdc.gov.my
InvestPenang – www.investpenang.gov.my
Penang Port – www.penangport.gov.my

Accommodation in Georgetown
Malaysia's own grand dame, the **Eastern & Oriental Hotel** (E&O for those in the know) was built by the industrious Sarkies Brothers, of Raffles Hotel Singapore fame. The grand colonial building sits prettily on the edge of the sea and the pool has a perfect view across the sea. Step into the shoes of famous former patrons such as Noël Coward, Douglas Fairbanks, Hermann Hesse, Rudyard Kipling and Somerset Maugham to discover what the fuss is all about.

Eastern & Oriental Hotel
10 Lebuh Farquhar
10200 Penang
Tel: +60 (4) 222 2000
Fax: +60 (4) 261 6333
Website: www.e-o-hotel.com
Rates from RM580 per night

G Hotel is a bold, beautiful creation that injects fresh new life into this sometimes sleepy state. It combines cool modernity with designer comfort. The hotel's convenient location overlooks Penang's most famous boulevard –

9

Gurney Drive. This means it is minutes to the sea and the shopping and dining attractions along the promenade.

G Hotel
168A Persiaran Gurney
10250 Penang
Malaysia
Tel: +60 (4) 238 0000
Fax: +60 (4) 238 0088
Website: www.ghotel.com.my
Rates from RM300 per night

Traders Hotel, Penang has 443 well-appointed guestrooms and suites in a contemporary style inspired by Malaysian designs. All rooms offer scenic Penang Bridge or city views through its well-placed and expansive bay windows.

Traders Hotel, Penang
Magazine Road
10300 Penang
Malaysia
Tel: +60 (4) 262 2622
Fax: +60 (4) 262 6526
Website: www.shangri-la.com
Rates from RM275 per night

Cheong Fatt Tze Mansion is a destination in itself. Believed to be one of only three surviving Chinese buildings of this magnitude (38 rooms, 5 granite-paved courtyards, 7 staircases and 220 windows), it is certainly the best preserved outside of China. In 2000, the Cheong Fatt Tze Mansion received the inaugural Unesco Asia Pacific Heritage Conservation Award, selected as the 'Most Excellent Project' in Asia Pacific following its RM7.6 million restoration. Rooms here are charming and special, littered with antique 'heirlooms'.

Cheong Fatt Tze Mansion
14, Leith Street
10200 Penang
Malaysia
Tel: +60 (4) 262 0006
Fax: +60 (4) 262 5289
Website: www.cheongfatttzemansion.com
Rates from RM320 per night

9

Accommodation in Batu Feringgi

Lone Pine Hotel is a wonderful beach retreat, with most of its 50 guest rooms facing the sea and shaded by a veil of lofty casuarina trees. Famous for its view of the sunset, it remains a perennial favourite for locals and visitors alike.

Lone Pine Hotel
97, Batu Ferringhi
11100 Penang
Malaysia
Tel: +60 (4) 881 1511/ 12
Fax: +60 (4) 881 1282
Website: www.lonepinehotel.com
Rates from RM230 per night

Shangri La Rasa Sayang Resort and Spa Penang takes its name from an old Malay folk song that also means 'a feeling of love'. With a long history in Penang, the Rasa Sayang is firmly etched in the minds of many locals as the benchmark for luxury beach resorts in Malaysia.

Shangri La Rasa Sayang Resort and Spa Penang
Batu Feringgi Beach
Batu Feringgi
Penang 11100
Malaysia
Tel: +60 (4) 888 8888
Fax: +60 (4) 881 1800
Website: www.shangri-la.com
Rates from RM595 per night

Melaka

Reputed to be the birthplace of Malaysia, Melaka's (also Malacca) 600-year-old history has seen the city state pass through the hands of colonial superpowers such as the Portuguese, Dutch and British. Throughout its early history, Melaka has flourished because of its activities as the leading port along the international spice trade route. The early exposure to globalisation has created a unique cultural and social history, evident in many of the remaining artefacts and the city's buildings. Designated a World Heritage Site, it is no wonder that the main source of revenue for this city is tourism.

9

Famous historical sites in the state include the **A Famosa, Stadthuys, St Paul's Church, St John's Fort** and the **Hang Tuah and Hang Jebat Mausoleums**. Antique lovers will find Jonker Street with its myriad of shops to be an intriguing place to hunt and bargain for treasures of the past.

The state measures only 1,650 square kilometres (1.3% of Malaysia's total land mass) and has hardly any natural resources. It is divided into three districts: Central Melaka, Alor Gajah and Jasin. The offshore Pulau Besar, Pulau Upeh and Tanjung Tuan are also parts of Melaka.

To ensure development, the state started to garner foreign investments as early as the 70s. Today there are 23 industrial estates with around 500 factories invested in by companies from the United States, Germany, Japan, Taiwan and also Singapore. Most of these factories are involved in the manufacturing sector, namely: the manufacturing of food and consumer products; high-tech weaponry and automotive components; and electronic and computer parts.

9

Investment projects

The Tanjung Kling and Batu Berendam areas are Free Trade Zones where imported materials used in manufacture are tax-free. New investment projects include the 140 acres in Pegoh, Alor Gajah, earmarked for the production of defence trucks by DRH-Hicom, and the first toxicology laboratory, valued at RM4.2 million, in Ayer Keroh. The latter is a direct result of the strong presence of high quality tertiary institutions that focus on technology and biomedical sciences.

Contacts

Invest Melaka – www.invest-melaka.com.my
Melaka State Development Corporation –
www.pknm.com
Multimedia University – www.mmu.edu.my
MARA University of Technology – www.uitm.edu.my
University Teknikal Malaysia Milaca –
www.utem.edu.my
Melaka Institute of Biotechnology – www.mib.gov.my

Accommodation

The Majestic Malacca is made up of an old mansion, which dates back to the 1920s, and a newly-constructed wing that carefully mirrors the original architecture. The result is a harmonious experience which satisfies the nostalgic craving while ensuring every modern convenience.

The Majestic Malacca
188 Jalan Bunga Raya
Malacca 75100
Malaysia
Tel: +60 (6) 289 8000
Fax: +60 (6) 289 8080
Website: www.majesticmalacca.com
Rates from RM859 per night

Holiday Inn Melaka is the city's newest hotel with a view of the Straits of Melaka. It is a basic business hotel that gets a mention here because of the dearth of well-maintained mid-range options in this city.

Holiday Inn Melaka
Jalan Syed Abdul Aziz
Melaka 75000
Malaysia
Tel: +60 (6) 285 9000
Fax: +60 (6) 285 9111
Website: www.ichotelsgroup.com
Rates from RM262 per night

Johor Bahru

The capital city of Johor State, Johor Bahru (also Johor Baru/Baharu), dubbed 'JB' by the locals, was founded in 1855 by Temenggong Daeng Ibrahim, a Malay chief, who promptly installed himself as the Sultan of Johor. But it was his son Sultan Abu Bakar who gave the fishing village its current name, and is now known as the 'Father of Modern Johor'. Much of the success Johor enjoys today can be traced directly to Sultan Abu Bakar's acumen when he persuaded British and Chinese entrepreneurs to invest in agricultural estates in the area.

While JB is not as picturesque as Penang or Melaka, it remains a favourite stopover for visitors. Indulge in some retail therapy at one of the shopping outlets or follow the heels of the intrepid food lovers. Start at the old part of town around **Jalan Wong Ah Fook** and explore the Hindu temple and old parts of town around Kotaraya. The **Sultan Abu Bakar Royal Palace Museum,** where various art collections, artefacts and many items related to Johor's historical heritage are stored, is definitely worth a visit. Just a stone's throw away, perched on a hilltop is the **Sultan Abu Bakar Mosque,** regarded as one of the most beautiful mosques in Malaysia.

Johor Bahru is the southernmost city of the Eurasian mainland, and right across the narrow Johor Straits lies Singapore. The two cities are connected by the Johor-Singapore Causeway, which is just over a kilometre long. From here Malaysia receives about 60% of the foreign tourists, earning Johor Bahru the title of 'Malaysia's Southern Gateway'. The city is served by Senai International Airport located 20km away. The airport is a secondary hub for low-cost carrier AirAsia.

9

With a population of approximately 876,000 in the city, 1.73 million in the greater metropolitan area, Johor Bahru is the fourth most populated city in Malaysia. The city is an important industrial, logistical and commercial centre in southern Malaysia. Its major industries include electronics, a petrochemical refinery and shipbuilding. The Port of Tanjung Pelepas is Malaysia's biggest trans-shipment hub, while the Pasir Gudang Port is the country's most important commodity and mineral resources seaports. Light to medium industrial areas are concetrated north and north-west of the metropolitan area in Tebrau, Tampoi, Senai, Skudai and Kulai.

Even though its industries are well-developed in their own right, Johor Bahru is often regarded as Singapore's hinterland, with many of Singapore's companies based here. Meanwhile a significant number of Malaysians residing in JB choose to commute daily to work in Singapore's factories for the higher wages. On the other side of the scale, bargain-loving Singaporeans arrive into JB in droves to take advantage of the stronger Singapore dollar, creating a highly developed retail scene, which many believe to be out of reach of the average JB resident. This tips the delicate socio-economic balance, resulting in higher crime rates in the recent years.

Contacts

Iskandar Regional Development Authority – www.irda.com.my

Johor Bahru City Council – www.mbjb.gov.my

Johor Corporation – www.jcorp.com.my

Port of Tanjung Pelepas – www.ptp.com.my

Johor Bahru Community Portal – www.johorbahru.com.my

Accommodation

The Puteri Pacific Johor Bahru is the city's most central business hotel and offers 500 guest rooms, suites and full-service apartments that are basic but comfortable.

The Puteri Pacific Johor Bahru
Jalan Abdullah Ibrahim
The Kotaraya
80730 Johor Bahru
Malaysia
Tel: +60 (7) 219 9999
Fax: +60 (7) 219 9998
Website: www.puteripacific.com
Rates from RM265 per night

East Malaysia

The states of Sabah and Sarawak are located across the South China Sea in Borneo. The states are large but many areas are still undeveloped or are coastal or mountainous regions. While East Malaysia is less populated and relatively less developed than West Malaysia, it has notably more natural resources, significantly, oil and gas reserves.

Kota Kinabalu

Kota Kinabalu, the capital of Sabah, is located on the north-west coast of the island of Borneo. Originally known as Jesselton, it was founded by the British North Borneo Company on the site of a local fishing village and transformed into a harbour and port. The entire town was razed during the second world war to prevent Jesselton falling into Japanese hands, but it was eventually rebuilt into what it is today. Its current name 'Kota Kinabalu', takes its name from the majestic Kinabalu Mountain, one of the highest peaks in South East Asia.

The state capital has many places of interest. The **Tunku Abdul Rahman Park**, adjacent to the city, is one of the top tourist destinations, perfect for relaxing, snorkelling and a wide variety of water sports. Other places of interest include the **Signal Hill Observatory** and the **State Mosque**. The **State Museum**, built to reflect the longhouse architecture of the Murut and Rungus people, offers an anthropological look into the history of its residents. Most visitors overlook these sites in the city because of one colossal reason – **Mount Kinabalu** is the only sight they have their eyes on.

With an estimated population of 532,129 in the city and 700,000 in the surrounding areas, Kota Kinabalu is the largest urban centre in Sabah and the sixth largest in Malaysia. KK, as the city is known by locals, is acquiring a sizeable reputation as a major tourist destination, offering a gateway into the intoxicating natural beauty available in Borneo. Kota Kinabalu International Airport serves the city and is located about 8km south-west of the city centre. It is the second busiest airport in Malaysia after Kuala Lumpur International Airport

The city is also one of the major industrial and commercial centres in East Malaysia. The primary sectors of industry dominate the economy and manufacturing plants are mostly concentrated in the industrial estates of Likas, Kolombong and Inanam.

Contacts

Kota Kinabalu City Hall – www.dbkk.sabah.gov.my
Sabah Tourism – www.sabahtourism.com
Sabah Development Corridor – www.sdc.net.my
Sabah Ports Authority – www.lpps.sabah.gov.my

Accommodation

Mercure Kota Kinabalu is a new hotel that is also part of the 1 Borneo Shopping Paradise complex. This well-designed hotel is exactly what the city needs, and all that a business traveller needs in this city.

9

Kota Kinabalu

Mercure Kota Kinabalu
Jalan Sulaman Highway Tower A
00-01 Ground Floor
1Borneo Hypermall
88450 Kota Kinabalu
Malaysia
Tel: +60 (8) 848 5533
Fax: +60 (8) 848 5522
Website: www.mercure.com
Rates from RM166 per night

Shangri-La's Tanjung Aru Resort and Spa offers the
best of Sabah – white sandy beaches and unsurpassed
turquoise water. When your business takes you to a
coastal location, take the opportunity to check into
a room with an ocean view.

Shangri-La's Tanjung Aru Resort and Spa
20 Jalan Aru, Tanjung Aru
88100 Kota Kinabalu
Sabah
Malaysia
Tel: +60 (8) 832 7888
Fax   +60 (8) 832 7878
Website: www.shangri-la.com
Rates from RM620 per night

Kuching

Kuching is the capital city of Sarawak, the largest state
in Malaysia, located on Borneo Island. It is the fourth
largest city in the country and the most populated in East
Malaysia. Kuching is situated along the banks of the
Sarawak River, on the north-western part of the island of
Borneo. There are no official accounts for why the name
Kuching (an old spelling of "cat" in Bahasa Malay) was
chosen to avoid confusion with the fast-expanding
Kingdom of Sarawak in the early 1900s, thus leaving
room for much speculation and theorising.

Its early history, intrinsically linked to one James Brooke,
is a fascinating and inspiring tale. British adventurer
James Brooke sailed for Borneo when his initial attempts
to trade in the Far East failed and he arrived in the area
where Kuching stands in 1838. He helped the Sultan

9

of Brunei quell a tribal uprising and in the process was granted the title Rajah of Sarawak. Brooke began to establish and cement his rule over his personal Kingdom of Sarawak by reforming the laws and administration, suppressing piracy and tribal practices like headhunting. Given the status of Protectorate under the second Rajah's rule, the Brooke family ruled Sarawak until the Japanese Occupation in 1941. After the second world war, the third Rajah of Sarawak ceded Sarawak to the British Colonial Office for a sizeable pension, thus ending the rule of the 'White Rajahs'.

Kuching is known for its cultural heritage and proudly proclaims itself the most multicultural city in Malaysia. Coupled with the architectural legacy of the Rajah dynasty, Kuching, nicknamed "Cat City", is a captivating destination. Interesting landmarks and sites are the **Astana** (the Rajah's former palace), **Fort Margherita**, **Tua Pek Kong temple**, the **Old Courthouse** and **Main Bazaar**. However, the main draws of Kuching are located just outside the city, in the form of national parks such as Bako, wildlife found in sanctuaries such as the Semenggoh Orang-Utan Rehabilitation Centre and traditional longhouse villages located further up the river offering a glimpse into everyday tribal life. Kuching is famous for its intense and beautiful sunsets that is often cited as some of the most beautiful in the world. Kuching International Airport is Sarawak's main international airport and is situated 11km south of the city.

9

The mainstays of the Sarawakian economy are its natural resources, chiefly natural gas and LPG. Sarawak is also one of the world's largest exporters of tropical hardwood timber and is the major contributor to Malaysian exports. The industrial landscape of Kuching reflects this trend, although efforts have been made to diversify and transform its economy into a more industrialised one.

Sama Jaya Free Industrial Zone, located eight kilometres from Kuching has attracted several multinational companies to base their high-tech manufacturing operations that producing electrical and electronic components here. Slightly further afield, light and medium industries are located in the Demak Laut Industrial Park and Kota Samarahan Industrial Estate.

Kuching is also home to many prestigious institutions of higher education, including the international campus of Australian-based Swinburne University of Technology.

Contacts

The Council of the City of Kuching South –
www.mbks.gov.my
Kuching North City Hall – www.dbku.gov.my
Kuching Port Authority – www.kpa.gov.my
Sarawak Government Website – www.sarawak.gov.my
Sarawak Economic Development Corporation –
www.sedc.com.my
Sarawak Development Institute – www.sdi.com.my
Sarawak Timber Industry Development
www.sarawaktimber.org.my

Accommodation

Four Points by Sheraton Kuching is one of the newest hotel development-designed to tap into the region's growth potential. Its inception finally enables Kuching to offer the high standards that discerning international travellers have come to expect.

Four Points by Sheraton Kuching
Lot 3186-3187 Block 16 KCLD
Jalan Lapangan Terbang Baru
Kuching 93350
Malaysia
Tel: +60 (82) 466 666
Fax: +60 (82) 466 888
Website: www.starwoodhotels.com
Rates unavailable at time of print

Hilton Kuching Hotel is a favourite oldie that provides good comfortable rooms. The hotel is in good condition and is well-maintained, which is definitely well-appreciated by its ever-returning local business guests and visiting dignitaries.

Hilton Kuching Hotel
Jalan Tunku Abdul Rahman
Kuching 93100
Malaysia
Tel: +60 (82) 248 200
Fax: +60 (82) 428 984
Website: www1.hilton.com
Rates from RM399 per night

9

a break from business

10

a break from business

10

Things to do and see in some
cities within Malaysia

There are few places in the world where business travelling can be as perfectly combined with leisure as Malaysia. A highly-developed tourist destination offering a tremendous diversity of activities and destination choices, Malaysia is quite simply the most pleasurable country to find yourself in with some time to spare, away from the demands of your business world.

Kuala Lumpur

Apart from the interesting sights and areas already mentioned in Chapter 8 which you can visit in the evenings or during the hours you steal between meetings and appointments, here is a list of sights and activities for those extending their stay for more than a day beyond their business commitments.

Petronas Twin Towers and surrounds

Most visitors are content with just a few snapshots of the impressive towers with their unique structural form with Moorish and Islamic influences, but the most famous landmark in Malaysia deserves a closer look. Visitors can actually visit the skybridge for free (limited to 1,300 persons per day). Located between the towers at the podium level, you can find the Dewan Filharmonik PETRONAS (PETRONAS Philharmonic Hall), a venue that was a gift from the state-owned oil company. Book a ticket to attend an evening's performance by the world-class Malaysian Philharmonic Orchestra. Another cultural gem, The Galeri PETRONAS, is a beautiful art gallery and is located on Level 3 of Suria KLCC. Visitors with family will appreciate PETROSAINS, an interactive science discovery centre, located on Level 4 of Suria KLCC.

Islamic Arts Museum (Muzium Kesenian Islam) is one of the most interesting museums in KL. The museum houses Islamic art through the ages and regularly changes its exhibitions to also feature artefacts related to the Muslim religion and Islamic culture.

National Museum contains cultural artefacts from the various ethnic communities of Malaysia and a sizeable natural history section showing the range of flora and fauna native to the country.

10

Sri Mahamariamman Temple is an elaborately-built Hindu temple that is the starting point of the yearly Thaipusam pilgrimage to the Batu Caves, where Hindu devotees haul portable altars pierced to their skin with 108 lances.

Central Market (Pasar Seni) used to be the old food and provisions market of central KL. Today it has been refurbished to house shops and stalls selling traditional and local crafts. This is a perfect place to take home some beautifully hand-woven silk wall-hangings or shop for souvenirs and gifts.

Batu Caves is a series of limestone outcrops located 13 kilometres outside KL. It is the focal point for the annual Thaipusam festival, usually held around February. Rising almost one hundred metres above the ground, Batu Caves actually consists of three main caves and a few smaller ones. The biggest, referred to as Cathedral Cave or Temple Cave, has a 100m-high ceiling, and features ornate Hindu shrines. To reach it, visitors have to climb a steep flight of 272 steps.

10

Destination hotels and resorts

With a vast expanse of coastlines, rivers and mountains, many luxury hotel operators have exquisite properties that are the perfect hideaways. This section's focus is not so much on the location of the destinations but on the hotels that are noteworthy destinations in their own right. Some of these hotels have already been mentioned in previous chapters, listed under the cities they are located in such as: the Eastern and Oriental in Penang, Carcosa Negara in Kuala Lumpur and Majestic Hotel in Melaka.

Four Season Resort Langkawi is a dreamy, lush tropical resort on the holiday island of Langkawi. It offers the unsurpassed Four Seasons experience in a unique Asian setting. The hotel's Andalusian design ethos is a touch of genius in this warm and inviting beach paradise. The island can be reach by air or by ferry-crossing from Penang, Kuala Kedah or Kuala Perlis.

The Datai is another amazing luxury resort on the island of Langkawi. Here, it is all about understated elegance, discreet villas nestled in the property's own rainforest and a sumptuous view of a private beach from the pool. This is truly one of those places you wish you would never have to leave.

JapaMala Resort can be found on the island of Tioman off the eastern shoreline of Peninsular Malaysia. Dubbed one of the 'Top 10 Ultra Boutique Hotels of the World' by luxury travel website globorati.com, it offers intimate teak villas overlooking the South China Sea, making it a hit for couples.

Tanjong Jara Resort is another beachfront sanctuary of luxury located near Kuala Trengganu. Steeped in age-old Malay traditions, this instalment of the Small Luxury Hotel of the World chain is designed to reflect the elegance and grandeur of 17th-century Malay palaces.

Destination beaches

While most business travellers will be content with being pampered in luxury hotels and a lavishly relaxing vacation, the more intrepid amongst you demand a different benchmark of paradise. Nothing short of the finest, whitest sandy beaches and clear, turquoise ocean waters teeming with marine life will gratify? Then these beach and/or diving destinations are for you.

Pulau Redang is one of the largest islands off the eastern coast of Malaysia in the state of Trengganu. Redang is one of nine islands, which form a marine park that offers pristine snorkelling and diving opportunities. The island is accessible by boats from Merang or Kuala Trenppanu; there is also a small airport with services operated by Berjaya Air from Singapore (Seletar Airport) and Kuala Lumpur (Sultan Abdul Aziz Shah Airport).

The highlights of Redang are the two historic shipwrecks just off the island and the sea turtle conservation programme that the public can contribute to or participate in. Accommodation comes in the form of large but generally lacklustre resorts and the usual basic but adequate diver shacks popular in these parts.

10

Perhentian Islands are also located in the state of Trengganu and belong to the same protected marine zone as Redang. These islands cater for a more 'balanced' crowd of families and holidaymakers rather than the predominately diving set that Redang attracts. Essentially made up of two islands, Perhentian Besar ('Big Perhentian') and Perhentian Kecil ('Small Perhentian'), both islands are fringed by white sand beaches, nearby reefs and crystalline waters.

The wide variety of corals and marine animals such as sea turtles, jellyfish, small sharks and reef-fish makes this island a haven for snorkellers and divers. Parts of Perhentian Kecil cater to a young backpacker crowd, creating amenities and an atmosphere that is both laid-back and vibrant.

The downside is that the season for these islands (and all other Peninsular east coast islands) is limited to the period between mid-February and late October due to the monsoonal climate. Outside this, the seas can be very rough and most (though not all) accommodation options are closed. Another deterrent is the fact that the only access to the islands is by boat from the fishing villages of Kuala Besut and Tok Bali. Local tour operators run fishing boats and speedboats several times a day and the boat journey takes 30 to 45 minutes.

Pulau Sipandan still remains undisputedly one of the world's best diving spots. It is located off the coast of Sabah in East Malaysia. The island is a protected marine park and features a one-of-a-kind diving experience. From the beach of Sipandan, one only needs to wade 20 metres into the shallow crystal waters to reach a dramatic drop where the reef wall starts and continues down for 1000-2000 metres. Here soft and hard corals and all types of reef and marine animals thrive. Sea turtles and white-tip reef sharks feature on virtually every dive, while hammerhead and leopard sharks make regular appearances.

Limited access, both in terms of getting there and the fact that there is a daily rota which allows for only 120 dives, may be the reason for its coveted pristine conditions. And, on top of that, divers can no longer stay on the island as the only resort has been closed to protect

10

the delicate natural treasure. So diving enthusiasts must contend with staying in basic lodgings in the surrounding coastal towns and islands of Semporna, Mabul or Kapalai. In 2000, the highly publicised kidnapping of 20 tourists from the area by Abu Sayyaf rebels also marred the island's tourism potential.

Nonetheless, the small number of visitors gives this island a truly exclusive feel. The most direct way to get to the island is to fly in to Tawau from Kuala Lumpur or Kota Kinabalu, then travel overland for about two hours to Semporna and finally catch an hour-long speedboat ride to arrive at Sipandan.

Eco- and Adventure Tourism

There are various lush and beautiful national parks in Malaysia. These parks are not of the usual low-density vegetation variety but are full, humid and, in many parts, inaccessible tropical jungles and rainforests. There are many different types of expeditions available, ranging from those where you hardly lose sight of the hotel to those where you are fully immersed in the jungle. You can also choose from the mode of transport – hiking, abseiling, rock climbing or white-water rafting. Here is a list of the more interesting or accessible national parks:

10

- Bako National Park, Sarawak – famed for its wildlife, especially bearded pigs and proboscis monkeys
- Batang Ai National Park, Sarawak – the Iban heartland, full of traditional longhouses
- Endau Rompin National Park, Johor
- Gunung Mulu National Park, Sarawak – fantastic limestones caves and karst formations
- Kinabalu National Park, Sabah – home of the 4,095 metre Gunung Kinabalu, the tallest peak in Borneo
- Taman Negara National Park – one of the world's oldest rainforests, spanning the Malaysian states of Kelantan, Pahang and Trengganu

See Tourism Malaysia for the detailed list of tour operators and resorts in these national parks (www.tourismmalaysia.gov.my).

Other Asian destinations

Alternatively, you can use Malaysia as your springboard to explore the rest of Asia. Low-cost carriers fly you directly to destinations throughout Asia. Most of the exciting destinations in Thailand, Vietnam, Macau and even Australia can be reached within five hours by flight. Nearby destinations include Singapore (only a 45-minute flight from Kuala Lumpur), Bali, Bangkok, Krabi and Phuket.

Tourism contacts

Hotel Bookings	– www.asiatravel.com
	– www.asiarooms.com
	– www.malaysia-hotels.net
	– www.kuala-lumpur.ws
Airlines	– www.malaysiaairlines.com
	– www.airasia.com
	– www.fireflyz.com.my
	– www.berjaya-air.com
	– www.silkair.com
	– www.singaporeair.com

10

appendix one

A1

appendix one

Useful telephone numbers and web addresses

The country code for Malaysia is 60

General emergencies

Police/Ambulance	Tel: 999
Civil Defence	Tel: 991
Fire & Rescue	Tel: 994
To Call from any Handphone	Tel: 112
Electrical Breakdown	Tel: 15454
Gas Emergency	Tel: 995
Water Woes (Selangor)	Tel: 1800 885 252

Telecommunication

(Telekom Lines Only)

Telephone, Datel & Telfax Faults	Tel: 100
Domestic Assisted Service	Tel: 101
Directory Service	Tel: 103
Telemessaging Service	Tel: 104
International Assisted Service	Tel: 108
Multilingual International Service (Mandarin)	Tel: 1981
Multilingual International Service (Japanese)	Tel: 1982
Data & Telex Faults	Tel: 1061

(Mobile Phone Services)

Maxis	Tel: 3 7492 2123
Celcom	Tel: 3 3630 8888
Digi	Tel: 1800 688 000

Airport

KLIA	Tel: 3 8776 4383
Alor Setar	Tel: 4 714 2788
Batu Berendam	Tel: 6 317 5860
Bintulu	Tel: 8 633 9163
Ipoh	Tel: 5 312 0848
Kota Bharu	Tel: 9 733 7400
Kota Kinabalu	Tel: 8 823 8555
Kuala Terengganu	Tel: 9 667 3666
Kuantan	Tel: 9 538 2023
Kuching	Tel: 82 454 242
Labuan	Tel: 87 415 015
Lahat Datu	Tel: 89 881 033
Langkawi	Tel: 4 955 1311

A1

Limbang	Tel: 85 214 979
Miri	Tel: 85 615 204
Pulau Pangkor	Tel: 5 685 2594
Pulau Pinang	Tel: 4 643 4411
Pulau Tioman	Tel: 9 419 1505
Sandakan	Tel: 89 660 405
Senai	Tel: 7 599 4500
Sibu	Tel: 84 307 770

Railway station

Kuala Lumpur	Tel: 3 2273 8000
Commuter	Tel: 3 2272 2828
Alor Setar	Tel: 4 733 1798
Arau	Tel: 4 986 1225
Bukit Mertajam	Tel: 4 539 2660
Butterworth	Tel: 4 331 2796
Gemas	Tel: 7 948 1026
Gua Musang	Tel: 9 912 1226
Ipoh	Tel: 5 254 7987
Jerantut	Tel: 9 266 2219
Johor Bahru	Tel: 7 223 4727
Kampar	Tel: 5 465 1489
Kluang	Tel: 7 771 0954
Kuala Krai	Tel: 9 966 6224
Kuala Lipis	Tel: 9 312 1341
Kuala Kangsar	Tel: 5 766 1094
Mentakab	Tel: 9 277 1002
Padang Besar	Tel: 4 949 0231
Pasir Mas	Tel: 9 790 9025
Pulau Pinang	Tel: 4 261 0290
Segamat	Tel: 7 931 1021
Seremban	Tel: 6 761 1708
Taiping	Tel: 5 807 5584
Tampin	Tel: 6 411 1034
Tapah Road	Tel: 5 418 1345
Tumpat	Tel: 9 725 7232
Wakaf Bharu	Tel: 9 719 6986

Immigration department

KLIA	Tel: 3 8776 8018
Kuala Lumpur	Tel: 3 2095 5077
Alor Setar	Tel: 4 733 3302
Ipoh	Tel: 5 254 9316
Johor Bahru	Tel: 7 224 4255
Kangar	Tel: 4 976 2636

A1

Kota Bharu	Tel: 9 748 2120
Kota Kinabalu	Tel: 88 280 700
Kuantan	Tel: 9 514 2155
Kuching	Tel: 82 245 661
Labuan	Tel: 87 412 298
Melaka	Tel: 6 292 3300
Padang Besar	Tel: 4 949 0350
Seremban	Tel: 6 762 0000
Pulau Pinang	Tel: 4 261 5122
Shah Alam	Tel: 3 5519 0653
Terengganu	Tel: 9 622 1424
Wilayah Persekutuan Kuala Lumpur	
	Tel: 3 2698 0377

Info lines

Time Announcement (Telekom)	Tel: 1051
Weather Forecast (Telekom)	Tel: 1052
MAS Call Centre	Tel: 1300 883 000

Road and transport

Touch 'N Go	Tel: 3 7628 5115
PLUS Line	Tel: 1800 880 000
KESAS	Tel: 3 5633 7188
LITRAK	Tel: 3 7494 7333
SPRINT	Tel: 3 7960 2000
AAM	Tel: 1800 880 808
KLIA Express	Tel: 3 2267 8000
KL Monorail	Tel: 3 2273 1888
PUTRA LRT	Tel: 1800 388 228
STAR LRT	Tel: 3 4294 9000

A1

Foreign diplomatic missions in Malaysia

AFGHANISTAN
Embassy of the Islamic State of Afghanistan
Level 2, Wisma Chinese Chamber, 258 Jalan Ampang,
50450 Kuala Lumpur
Tel: 34256 9400   Fax: 3 4256 6400

ALBANIA
Embassy of the Republic of Albania
No. 2952, Jalan Bukit Ledang, Off Jalan Duta
50480 Kuala Lumpur
Tel: 3 2093 7808   Fax: 3 2093 7359

ALGERIA
Embassy of the People's Democratic Republic of Algeria
No. 5, Jalan Mesra, Off Jalan Damai, 55000 Kuala Lumpur
Tel: 3 2148 8159   Fax: 3 2148 8154

ARGENTINA
Embassy of the Argentine Republic
3, Jalan Semantan Dua, Damansara Heights, 50490
Kuala Lumpur
Tel: 3 2095 0176   Fax: 3 2095 2706

AUSTRALIA
Australian High Commission
No. 6, Jalan Yap Kwan Seng, 50450 Kuala Lumpur Tel:
3 2146 5555   Fax: 3 2141 4323

AUSTRIA
Austrian Embassy
7th Floor, MUI Plaza Building, Jalan P. Ramlee, 50250
Kuala Lumpur
Tel: 3 2148 4277   Fax: 3 2148 9813

BANGLADESH
High Commission for the Peoples' of Bangladesh
Block 1, Lorong Damai 7, Jalan Damai, 55000 Kuala
Lumpur
Tel: 3 2148 7940   Fax: 3 2141 3381

BELGIUM
Royal Embassy of Belgium
8A, Jalan Ampang Hilir, 55000 Kuala Lumpur
Tel: 3 4252 5733   Fax: 3 4252 7922

BOSNIA AND HERZEGOVINA
Embassy of Bosnia and Herzegovina
JKR 854, Jalan Bellamy, 50460 Kuala Lumpur
Tel: 3 2144 0353   Fax: 3 2142 6025

BRAZIL
Embassy of the Federative Republic of Brazil
22 Persiaran Damansara Endah, Damansara Heights,
50490 Kuala Lumpur
Tel: 3 2094 8020   Fax: 3 2094 5086

A1

BRUNEI DARUSSALAM
High Commission of Brunei Darussalam
Suite 19-01, Tingkat 19, Menara Tan & Tan, 207 Jalan
Tun Razak, 50400 Kuala Lumpur
Tel: 3 2161 2800   Fax: 3 2163 1302

CAMBODIA
Royal Embassy of the Kingdom of Cambodia
No. 46, Jalan U-Thant, 55000 Kuala Lumpur
Tel: 3 4257 3711   Fax: 3 4257 1157

CANADA
Canadian High Commission
17th Floor, Menara Tan& Tan, 207 Jalan Tun Razak,
50400 Kuala Lumpur
Tel: 3 2718 3333   Fax: 3 2718 3376

CHILE
Embassy of Chile
Wisma Selangor Dredging, 8th Floor West Block, 142-C
Jalan Ampang, 50450 Kuala Lumpur
Tel: 3 2161 62 3   Fax: 3 2162 2219

CHINA
Embassy of the People's Republic of China
229, Jalan Ampang, 50450 Kuala Lumpur
Tel: 3 2142 8595   Fax: 3 2142 4552

COLOMBIA
Embassy of the Republic of Colombia
Business Suite 19A-26-1, Level 26, UOA Centre, 19,
Jalan Pinang, 50450 Kuala Lumpur
Tel: 3 2164 5488   Fax: 3 2164 5487

CROATIA
Embassy of the Republic of Croatia
No. 3 Jalan Mengkuang, Off Jalan Rhu, Ampang, 55000
Kuala Lumpur
Tel: 3 4253 5340   Fax: 3 4253 5217

CUBA
Embassy of Cuba
20 Lingkungan U Thant, Off Jalan U Thant, 55000
Kuala Lumpur
Tel: 3 4251 6808   Fax: 3 4252 0428

A1

CZECH REPUBLIC
Embassy of the Czech Republic
32, Jalan Mesra, Off Jalan Damai , 55000 Kuala Lumpur
Tel: 3 2142 7185   Fax: 3 2141 2727

DENMARK
Royal Danish Embassy
Wisma Denmark, 22nd Floor, 86 Jalan Ampang, 50450
Kuala Lumpur
Tel: 3 2032 2001   Fax: 3 2032 2012

ECUADOR
Embassy of the Republic of Ecuador
10th Floor, West Block, Wisma Selangor Dredging, 142-
C Jalan Ampang, 50450 Kuala Lumpur
Tel: 3 2163 5078   Fax: 3 2163 5096

EGYPT
Embassy of the Arab Republic of Egypt
28, Lingkungan U Thant, Off Jalan U Thant, 55000
Kuala Lumpur
Tel: 3 4256 8184   Fax: 3 4257 3515

EUROPEAN COMMISSION
Delegation of the European Commission
Suite 23.01, Menara Tan & Tan, 207 Jalan Tun Razak,
50400 Kuala Lumpur
Tel: 3 2733 7373   Fax: 3 2723 7337

FIJI ISLANDS
High Commission of the Republic of the Fiji Islands
Level 2, Menara Chan, 138 Jalan Ampang, 50450 Kuala
Lumpur
Tel: 3 2732 3335   Fax: 3 2732 7555

FINLAND
Embassy of Finland
Wisma Chinese Chamber 5th Floor, 258 Jalan Ampang
50450 Kuala Lumpur
Tel: 3 4257 7746   Fax: 3 4257 7793

FRANCE
Embassy of France
192-196 Jalan Ampang, 50450 Kuala Lumpur
Tel: 3 2053 5500   Fax: 3 2053 5501

A1

GERMANY
German Embassy Kuala Lumpur
26th Floor, Menara Tan & Tan, 207 Jalan Tun Razak,
50400 Kuala Lumpur
Tel: 3 2170 9666   Fax: 3 2161 9800/01

GHANA
High Commission of the Republic of Ghana
14 Ampang Hilir, Off Jalan Ampang, 55000 Kuala Lumpur
Tel: 3 4252 6995   Fax: 3 4257 8698

GUINEA
Embassy of the Republic of Guinea
No. 5, Jalan Kedondong, Off Jalan Ampang Hilir, Kuala
Lumpur
Tel: 3 4257 6500   Fax: 3 4251 1500

HUNGARY
Embassy of the Republic of Hungary
Suite 30C, 30th Floor, Empire Tower, City Square
Centre, Jalan Tun Razak, 50400 Kuala Lumpur
Tel: 3 2163 7914   Fax: 3 2163 7918

INDIA
High Commission of India
No. 2 Jalan Taman Duta, Off Jalan Duta, 50480 Kuala
Lumpur
Tel: 3 2093 3504   Fax: 3 2093 3507

INDONESIA
Embassy of the Republic of Indonesia
233 Jalan Tun Razak, 50400 Kuala Lumpur
Tel: 3 2142 1354   Fax: 3 21417908

IRAN
Embassy of the Islamic Republic of Iran
No. 1, Lorong U-Thant Satu, Off Jalan U-Thant, 55000
Kuala Lumpur
Tel: 3 4251 4824   Fax: 3 4256 2904

IRAQ
Embassy of the Republic of Iraq
2 Jalan Langgak Golf, Off Jalan Tun Razak, 55000
Kuala Lumpur
Tel: 3 2148 0555   Fax: 3 2141 4331

A1

IRELAND
Embassy of Ireland
Ireland House
The Amp Walk, 218 Jalan Ampang, 50450 Kuala Lumpur
Tel: 3 2161 2963   Fax: 3 2161 3427

ITALY
Embassy of the Republic of Italy
99 Jalan U Thant, 55000 Kuala Lumpur
Tel: 3 4256 5122   Fax: 3 4257 3199

JAPAN
Embassy of Japan
No.11, Persiaran Stonor, Off Jln Tun Razak, 50450
Kuala Lumpur
Tel: 3 2142 7044   Fax: 3 2167 2314

JORDAN
Embassy of the Hashemite Kingdom of Jordan
No.2 Jalan Kedondong, Off Jalan Ampang Hilir, 55000
Kuala Lumpur
Tel: 3 4252 1268   Fax: 3 4252 8610

KAZAKHSTAN
Embassy of the Republic of Kazakhstan
Box # 21, Wisma Selangor Dredging, 3rd Floor, South
Block, 142-A, Ampang, 50540 Kuala Lumpur
Tel: 3 2166 4144   Fax: 3 2166 8553

KENYA
High Commission of the Republic of Kenya
Empire Tower Building , Unit 38C, 38th Floor, 182 Jalan
Tun Razak, 50400 Kuala Lumpur
Tel: 3 2164 5015   Fax: 3 2164 5017

KOREA (NORTH)
Embassy of the Democratic People's Republic of Korea
No. 4, Persiaran Madge, Off Jalan U Thant , 55000
Kuala Lumpur
Tel: 3 4256 9913   Fax: 3 4256 9933

KOREA (SOUTH)
Embassy of the Republic of Korea
No. 9 and 11, Jalan Nipah, Off Jalan Ampang, 55000
Kuala Lumpur
Tel: 3 4251 2336   Fax: 3 4252 1425

A1

KUWAIT
Embassy of the State of Kuwait
229 Jalan Tun Razak, 50400 Kuala Lumpur
Tel: 3 2141 0033   Fax: 3 2142 6126

KYRGYZSTAN
Embassy of the Kyrgyz Republic
No. 10, Lorong Damai 9, 55000 Kuala Lumpur
Tel: 3 2164 9862   Fax: 3 2163 2024

LAOS
Embassy of the Lao People's Democratic Republic
No. 25, Jalan Damai, 55000 Kuala Lumpur
Tel: 3 2148 7059   Fax: 3 2145 0080

LIBYA
The People's Bureau of the Great Socialist People's
Libyan Arab Jamahiriya, No. 6, Jalan Madge, Off Jalan
U Thant, 55000 Kuala Lumpur
Tel: 3 2141 1293   Fax: 3 2141 3549

LUXEMBOURG
Embassy of the Grand Duchy of Luxembourg
Suite 16), 16th Floor, Menara Keck Seng , 2,
Jalan Bukit Bintang, 55100 Kuala Lumpur
Tel: 3 2143 3134   Fax: 3 2143 3157

A1

MAURITIUS
High Commission of the Republic of Mauritius
Wisma Selangor Dredging, Lot W17-B1 & C1, 17th
Floor, West Block, 142-C, Jalan Ampang, 50450 Kuala
Lumpur
Tel: 3 2163 6306   Fax: 3 2163 6294

MEXICO
Embassy of Mexico
Menara Tan & Tan , 22nd Floor, 207 Jalan Tun Razak,
50400 Kuala Lumpur
Tel: 3 2164 6362   Fax: 3 2164 0964

MOROCCO
Embassy of the Kingdom of Morocco
Box 9, Wisma Selangor Dredging, 3rd Floor East Block,
142-B Jalan Ampang, 50450 Kuala Lumpur
Tel: 3 2161 0701   Fax: 3 2162 3081

MYANMAR
Embassy of the Union of Myanmar
No. 12, Jalan Rhu, Off Jalan Ampang Hilir, 55000 Kuala
Lumpur
Tel: 3 4256 0280   Fax: 3 4256 8320

NAMIBIA
High Commission of Namibia
Suite 15-01, Level 15, Menara HLA, No. 3, Jalan Kia
Peng, 50450 Kuala Lumpur
Tel: 3 2164 6520   Fax: 3 2168 8790

NEPAL
The Royal Nepalese Embassy
Suite 13A-01, 13th A Floor, Wisma MCA, 163 Jalan
Ampang, 50450 Kuala Lumpur
Tel: 3 2164 5934   Fax: 3 2164 8659

NETHERLANDS
Royal Netherlands Embassy
7th Floor, South Block. The Ampwalk, 218, Jalan
Ampang, 50480 Kuala Lumpur
Tel: 3 2168 6200   Fax: 3 2168 6240

NEW ZEALAND
New Zealand High Commission
21st Floor, Menara IMC, No. 8, Jalan Sultan Ismail,
50250 Kuala Lumpur
Tel: 3 2078 2533   Fax: 3 2078 0387

NIGERIA
High Commission of the Federal Republic of Nigeria
No. 85, Jalan Ampang Hilir, 55000 Kuala Lumpur
Tel: 3 4251 7843   Fax: 3 4252 4302

NORWAY
The Royal Norwegian Embassy
53rd Floor, Empire Tower, Jalan Tun Razak, 50400
Kuala Lumpur
Tel: 3 2175 0300   Fax: 3 2175 0308

OMAN
Embassy of the Sultanate of Oman
No. 109, Jalan U-Thant, 55000 Kuala Lumpur
Tel: 3 4257 7378   Fax: 3 4257 1400

A1

PAKISTAN
High Commission for the Islamic Republic of Pakistan
132, Jalan Ampang, 50450 Kuala Lumpur
Tel: 3 2161 8877   Fax: 3 2164 5958

PALESTINE
Embassy of the State of Palestine
63, Jalan U Thant, 55000 Kuala Lumpur
Tel: 3 4256 8905   Fax: (04)4252 9711

PAPUA NEW GUINEA
Papua New Guinea High Commission
No. 11 Jalan Lingkungan U-Thant, Off Jalan U-Thant,
55000 Kuala Lumpur
Tel: 3 4257 5405   Fax: 3 4257 6203

PERU
Embassy of the Republic of Peru
Wisma Selangor Dredging
6th. Floor South Block, 142-A, Jalan Ampang, 50450
Kuala Lumpur
Tel: 3 2163 3034   Fax: 3 2163 3039

PHILIPPINES
Embassy of the Republic of the Philippines
No. 1 Changkat Kia Peng, 50450 Kuala Lumpur
Tel: 3 2148 4233   Fax: 3 2148 3576

POLAND
Embassy of the Republic of Poland
495 4 1/2 Miles Jalan Ampang, 68000 Ampang,
Selangor Darul Ehsan
Tel: 3 4257 6733   Fax: 3 4257 0123

ROMANIA
Embassy of Romania
114, Jalan Damai, Off Jalan Ampang, 55000 Kuala
Lumpur
Tel: 3 2142 3172   Fax: 3 2144 8713

RUSSIA
Embassy of the Russian Federation
263, Jalan Ampang, 50450 Kuala Lumpur
Tel: 3 4256 0009   Fax: 3 4257 6091

A1

SAUDI ARABIA
Royal Embassy of Saudi Arabia
4th Floor, Wisma Chinese Chamber, No. 258, Jalan
Ampang, 50450 Kuala Lumpur
Tel: 3 4257 9825   Fax: 3 4257 8751

SENEGAL
Embassy of the Republic of Senegal
No. 6, Lorong Damai 12, Off Jalan Damai, 55000 Kuala
Lumpur
Tel: 3 4256 7343   Fax: 3 4256 3205

SEYCHELLES
High Commission of the Republic of Seychelles
No. 50 (2nd Floor), Jln SS 19/1D, 47500 Subang Jaya,
Selangor Darul Ehsan
Tel: 3 5638 9881   Fax: 3 5638 0108

SINGAPORE
High Commission of the Republic of Singapore
209, Jalan Tun Razak, 50400 Kuala Lumpur
Tel: 3 2161 6277   Fax: 3 2161 6343

SLOVAKIA
Embassy of the Slovakia, Republic
11 Jalan U-Thant, 55000 Kuala Lumpur
Tel: 3 2115 0016   Fax: 3 2115 0014

SOUTH AFRICA
High Commission of the Republic of South Africa
No. 12, Lorong Titiwangsa 12, Taman Tasik Titiwangsa,
53200 Kuala Lumpur
Tel: 3 4026 5700   Fax: 3 4024 9896

SPAIN
Embassy of Spain
200, Jalan Ampang, 50450 Kuala Lumpur
Tel: 3 2142 8776   Fax: 3 2142 4582

SRI LANKA
High Commission of the Democratic Socialist Republic of
Sri Lanka,
No. 12, Jalan Keranji Dua, Off Jalan Kedondong
Ampang Hilir, 55000 Kuala Lumpur
Tel: 3 4256 8987   Fax: 3 2142 4582

A1

SUDAN
Embassy of the Republic of Sudan
No. 2 & 2A, Persiaran Ampang, Off Jalan Ru, 55000
Kuala Lumpur
Tel: 3 4256 9104   Fax: 3 4256 8107

SWAZILAND
High Commission of the Kingdom of Swaziland
Suite 22A, Menara Citibank, 165 Jalan Ampang, 50450
Kuala Lumpur
Tel: 3 2163 2511   Fax: 3 2163 3326

SWEDEN
Embassy of Sweden
6th Floor Bangunan Angkasa Raya, 123 Jalan Ampang,
50450 Kuala Lumpur
Tel: 3 2052 2550   Fax: 3 2148 6325

SWITZERLAND
Embassy of Switzerland
16, Persiaran Madge, 55000 Kuala Lumpur
Tel: 3 2148 0622   Fax: 3 2148 0935

SYRIAN ARAB REPUBLIC
Embassy of the Syrian Arab Republic
Suite 23, 23rd Floor, Menara Tan & Tan, 207 Jalan Tun
Razak, 50400 Kuala Lumpur
Tel: 3 2163 4110   Fax: 3 2163 4199

A1

TIMOR-LESTE
Embassy of the Democratic Republic of Timor-Leste
62, Jalan Ampang Hilir, 55000 Kuala Lumpur
Tel: 3 4256 2078   Fax: 3 4256 2016

THAILAND
Royal Thai Embassy
206, Jalan Ampang, 50450 Kuala Lumpur
Tel: 3 2148 8222   Fax: 3 2148 6527

TURKEY
Embassy of the Republic of Turkey
118, Jalan U Thant, 55000 Kuala Lumpur
Tel: 3 4257 2225   Fax: 3 4257 2227

UKRAINE
Embassy of Ukraine
22nd Floor, Menara Tan & Tan, 207 Jalan Tun Razak,
50400 Kuala Lumpur
Tel: 3 2166 9552   Fax: 3 2166 4371

UNITED ARAB EMIRATES
Embassy of the United Arab Emirates
No.1, Gerbang Ampang Hilir, Off Persiaran Ampang
Hilir, 55000 Kuala Lumpur
Tel: 3 4253 5221   Fax: 3 4253 5220

**UNITED KINGDOM OF GREAT BRITAIN
AND NORTHERN IRELAND**
British High Commission
185 Jalan Ampang, 50450 Kuala Lumpur
Tel: 3 2170 2200   Fax: 3 2170 2370

UNITED STATES OF AMERICA
Embassy of the United States of America
376 Jalan Tun Razak, 50400 Kuala Lumpur
Tel: 3 2168 5000   Fax: 3 2142 2207

URUGUAY
Embassy of the Republic of Uruguay
21, Jalan Taman U-Thant, Off Jalan U-Thant, 55000
Kuala Lumpur
Tel: 3 2143 3364   Fax: 3 2143 3723

UZBEKISTAN
Embassy of the Republic of Uzbekistan
No. 2, Jalan 12, Taman Tun Abdul Razak, 68000
Ampang, Selangor Darul Ehsan
Tel: 3 4253 3406   Fax: 3 4253 5406

VENEZUELA
Embassy of Bolivarian Republic of Venezuela
Suite 20-05, 20th Floor, Menara Tan & Tan, 207 Jalan
Tun Razak, 50400 Kuala Lumpur
Tel: 3 2163 3444   Fax: 3 2163 6819

VIETNAM
Embassy of the Socialist Republic of Vietnam
4, Persiaran Stonor, 50450 Kuala Lumpur
Tel: 3 2148 4534   Fax: 3 2148 3270

A1

YEMEN
Embassy of the Republic of Yemen
7, Jalan Kedondong, Off Jalan Ampang Hilir, 55000
Kuala Lumpur
Tel: 3 4251 1793   Fax: 3 4251 1794

ZIMBABWE
Embassy of the Republic of Zimbabwe
124, Jalan Sembilan, Taman Ampang Utama, 68000
Ampang, Selangor Darul Ehsan
Tel: 3 4251 6779   Fax: 3 4251 7252

Business councils and chambers of commerce

American Malaysian Chamber of Commerce
(AMCHAM)
11, Level 11, Amoda, 22 Jalan Imbi, 55100 Kuala
Lumpur
Tel: 3 2148 2407
Fax: 3 2142 8540
Website: www.amcham.com.my
Email: info@amcham.com.my

British Malaysian Chamber of Commerce (BMCC)
c/o British High Commission
185 Jalan Ampang, 50450 Kuala Lumpur
Tel: 3 2163 1784
Fax: 3 2163 1781
Website: www.bmcc.org.my

The Japanese Chamber of Trade & Industry Malaysia
(JACTIM)
Suite 6.01, 6th Floor, Regent Office Block, Peti #4, 160,
Jalan Bukit Bintang, 55100 Kuala Lumpur
Tel: 3 2142 7106
Fax: 3 2142 0483
Website: www.jactim.org.my
Email: jactim@jcci.com.my

Korea Trade Investment Promotion Agency, Kuala
Lumpur (KOTRA)
Korea Trade Center, Kuala Lumpur
(Korean Goverment Trade Representative)
9th Floor, MUI Plaza, 50250, Kuala Lumpur
Tel: 3 2142 0756

A1

Fax: 3 2142 2107
Website: www.kotrakl.com.my
Email: info@kotrakl.com.my

Malaysia Australia Business Council (MABC)
Quest Business Centre, 3rd Floor, Wisma RKT, No.2,
Jalan Raja Abdullah, 5 300 Kuala Lumpur
Tel: 3 2695 3121
Fax: 3 2695 3128
Website: www.mabc.org.my
Email: mabc@mabc.org.my

Malaysia Belgium-Luxembourg Business Council (MBLBC)
Menara Great Eastern, Suite 11.1, Level 11, No 3 Jalan
Ampang, 50450 Kuala Lumpur
Tel: 3 4252 7335
Fax: 3 4256 0277
Website: www.mblbc.com.my
Email: info@mblbc.com.my

Malaysia Canada Business Council (MCBC)
c/o UCSI, Lot 18113, Off Jalan Cerdas, Taman
Connaught, 56000 Cheras, Kuala Lumpur
Tel: 3 9101 8880
Fax: 3 9102 3606
Website: www.malaysia-canada.com
Email: mcbc_my@yahoo.com

Malaysia China Business Council (MCBC)
Asian Strategy & Leadership Institute.
1718, Jalan Ledang, Off Jalan Duta, 50480 Kuala Lumpur
Tel: 3 2093 5393
Fax: 3 2093 3078
Email: chaimee@po.jaring.my

Malaysian Chile Joint Business Council
17th Floor, Bangunan AmBank Group, Jalan Raja
Chulan, 50200 Kuala Lumpur.
Tel: 3 2078 3788
Fax: 3 2072 8411

Malaysia Danish Business Council (MDBC)
c/o Royal Danish Embassy, 2nd Floor, Wisma Denmark
Jalan Ampang, 50450 Kuala Lumpur
Tel: 3 2032 2001
Fax: 3 2032 2012

Malaysia Dutch Business Council (MDBC)
c/o Royal Netherlands Embassy
The AmpWalk, 7th Floor, South Block, 218 Jalan
Ampang, 50450 Kuala Lumpur
Tel: 3 7492 1077
Fax: 3 7492 5166
Website: www.mdbc.com.my
Email: info@mdbc.com.my

Malaysian Finnish Business Council (MFBC)
C11-4F, Jalan Ampang Utama 1/1, Off Jalan Ampang,
68000 Ampang, Selangor Darul Ehsan
Tel: 3 4251 1386
Fax: 3 4251 1534
Website: www.mfbc.org.my
Email: info@mfbc.org.my

Malaysian French Chamber of Commerce & Industry
(MFCCI)
Level 16, Menara KUB.com, Jalan Yap Kwan Seng,
50450 Kuala Lumpur
Tel: 3 2718 9888
Fax: 3 2718 9889
Email: mfcci@nasioncom.net

Malaysian German Chamber Of Commerce & Industry
(MGCC)
Suite 47.01, Level 47 Bangunan AMFinance, 8 Jalan Yap
Kwan Seng, 50450 Kuala Lumpur
Tel: 3 2078 3561
Fax: 3 2072 1198
Website: www.mgcc.com.my
Email: mgcc@mgcc.com.my

Malaysia India Joint Business Committee
37, Jalan Kia Peng, 50450 Kuala Lumpur
Tel: 3 2141 9600
Fax: 3 2141 3775
Email: enquiry@nccim.org.my

Malaysia New Zealand Business Council (MNZBC)
c/o New Zealand High Commission, Level 21, Menara
IMC, No. 8, Jalan Sultan Ismail, 50250 Kuala Lumpur
Tel: 3 2144 2422
Fax: 3 2144 1422

A1

Website: www.mnzbc.com.my
Email: mnzbc@mnzbc.com.my

Malaysia Norway Business Council (MNBC)
c/o Royal Norwegian Embassy,
P.O. Box 1 332, 50710 Kuala Lumpur
Tel: 3 2175 300
Fax: 3 2175 308
Website: www.mnbc.com.my
Email: mnbc@po.jaring.my

Malaysia Peru Joint Business Cooperation
17th Floor, Bangunan Ambank Group, Jalan Raja
Chulan, 50200 Kuala Lumpur.
Tel: 3 2078 3788
Fax: 3 2072 8411
Email: massa@po.jaring.my

Malaysian Philippines Business Council
Level 9, Grand Seasons Avenue, 72, Jalan Pahang, 53000
Kuala Lumpur.
Tel: 3 2698 9122
Fax: 3 2691 1779

Malaysia Poland Business Council (MPBC)
Tel: 3 4042 7886
Fax: 3 4043 0216

Malaysian Saudi Arabian Friendship Society
83, 18th Floor, Wisma Bumi Raya, Jalan Raja Laut, 5
350
Tel: 3 2693 1407
Fax: 3 2693 1816
Email: msfc@tm.net.my

Malaysia South Africa Business Council (MSABC)
Administrative Office, 54-1 Jalan Telawi, Bangsar Baru,
59100 Kuala Lumpur

Malaysian Swedish Business Association (MASBA)
c/o Embassy of Sweden, 6th Floor, Wisma Angkasa Raya,
123, Jalan Ampang, 54050 Kuala Lumpur
Tel: 3 2143 4101
Fax: 3 2143 4889
Website: www.masba.org
Email: swebiz@tm.net.my

A1

Swiss Malaysian Business Association (MSBA)
c/o Embassy of Switzerland
16 Persiaran Madge, 55000 Kuala Lumpur
Tel: 3 2162 9889
Fax: 3 2162 8410
Website: www.myswiss.org
Email: myswiss@tm.net.my

Taipeh Investors Association in Malaysia (TIAM)
CS/3B/20-5,Plaza Sentral,Jalan Stesen Sentral 5, 50470
Kuala Lumpur
Tel: 3 2274 6344
Fax: 3 2273 5366
Website: www.tiam.com.my
Email: tiammy@tm.net.my

Airlines in Malaysia

Aeroflot – Russian International Airlines
Tel: 3 2161 0231
Fax: 3 2161 7294
Website: www.aeroflot.org

AirAsia Berhand
Tel: 3 7884 9000
Tel: 1300 889 933
Fax: 3 7804 5430
Website: www.airasia.com.my

Air Canada
Tel: 3 2148 8596
Fax: 3 2148 1357
Website: www.aircanada.ca

Air France
Tel: 3 7712 4555
Fax: 3 7712 4556
Website: www.airfrance.com

Air India
Tel: 3 2142 0323
Fax: 3 2142 5834
Website: www.airindia.com

A1

Air Mauritius
Tel: 3 2142 9161
Fax: 3 2144 0230
Website: www.airmauritius.com

Asiana Airlines
Tel: 3 2144 2900
Fax: 3 2148 1357
Website: www.flyasiana.com

Austrian Airlines
Tel: 3 2148 6033
Fax: 3 2148 6033
Website: www.aua.com

Berjaya Air
Tel: 3 7847 6828
Fax: 3 7847 6228
Website: www.berjaya-air.com

Biman Bangladesh
Tel: 3 2148 3765
Fax: 3 2145 6860

British Airways
Tel: 3 2167 6188
Fax: 3 2167 6189
Website: www.britishairways.com

Cargolux Airlines International FA
Tel: 3 8787 3343
Fax: 3 8787 3319

Cathay Pacific
Tel: 3 2073 5101
Fax: 3 2072 4769
Website: www.cathaypacific.com

China Airlines
Tel: 3 2142 4125
Fax: 3 2141 8208
Website: www.china-airlines.com

China Eastern Airlines
Tel: (+607)334 4970
Fax: (+607)334 5088

A1

China Southern Airlines
Tel: 3 2163 9977
Fax: 3 2163 9911
Website: www.cs-air.com

Egyptair
Tel: 3 2145 6867
Fax: 3 2145 6873
Website: www.egyptair.com.eg

Emirates Airlines
Tel: 3 2072 5288
Fax: 3 2072 4788
Website: www.emirates.com

Eva Airways Corpration
Tel: 3 2161 7500
Fax: 3 2161 3596
Website: www.evaair.com

First Cambodia Airlines
Tel: 3 9283 5090
Fax: 3 9283 3669

Garuda Indonesia
Tel: 3 2162 1581
Fax: 3 2162 3435
Website: www.garuda-indonesia.com

Gulf Air
Tel: 3 2142 2060
Fax: 3 8776 4781
Website: www.gulfairco.com

Indian Airlines Limited
Tel: 3 4044 3055
Fax: 3 4044 6055

Iran Air
Tel: 3 2161 0411
Fax: 3 2162 2010
Website: www.iranair.com

Japan Airlines International Co Ltd
Tel: 3 2161 1740

A1

Fax: 3 2161 8216
Website: www.jal.co.jp

KLM Royal Dutch Airlines
Tel: 3 7712 4555
Fax: 3 7712 4556
Website: www.klm.com

Korean Airlines
Tel: 3 2142 8616
Fax: 3 2141 3703
Website: www.koreanair.com

Lion Airlines
Tel: 3 2713 9911
Fax: 3 2713 6611

Lufthansa German Airlines
Tel: 3 2161 4666
Fax: 3 2161 3079
Website: www.lufthansa.com

Malaysia Airlines
Tel: 3 7846 3000
Tel: 1 300 88 3000
Fax: 3 2162 9025
Website: www.malaysiaairlines.com

Merpati Nusantara Airlines
Tel: 3 2141 1411
Tel: 3 2144 1411

Myanmar Airways International
Tel: 3 2144 3077
Fax: 3 2142 9392
Website: www.maiair.com

Nippon Cargo Airlines
Tel: 3 2032 5393
Fax: 3 2032 5400

Pakistan International Airways
Tel: 3 2142 5444
Fax: 3 2141 8627
Website: www.piac.com.pk

A1

Philippines Airlines
Tel: 3 2141 0767
Fax: 3 2178 1357
Website: www.philippineair.com

Qatar Airways
Tel: 3 2141 8281
Fax: 3 2141 8117
Website: www.qatarairways.com

Royal Brunei Airlines Sdn Bh
Tel: 3 2070 6628
Fax: 3 2070 6899
Website: www.bruneiair.com

Royal Jordanian Airlines
Tel: 3 8776 4757
Fax: 3 8776 4755

Royal Nepal Airlines
Tel: 3 4045 6255
Fax: 3 4045 7255

Saudi Arabian Airlines
Tel: 3 2166 4488
Fax: 3 2166 3387
Website: www.saudiairlines.com

Scandinavian Airlines
Tel: 3 2142 6044
Fax: 3 2142 6123
Website: www.scandinavian.net

Singapore Airlines
Tel: 3 2698 7033
Fax: 3 2694 9818
Website: www.singaporeair.com

Sri Lankan Airlines
Tel: 3 2072 2833
Fax: 3 2078 8233
Website: www.srilankan.aero

Swiss International Airline
Tel: 3 2163 5885

A1

Fax: 3 2163 5880
Website: www.swiss.com

Thai Airways International
Tel: 3 2031 1900
Fax: 3 2032 5805
Website: www.thaiair.com

Transmile Air
Tel: 3 7846 9520
Fax: 3 7846 9527

Turkish Airline GSA Kuala Lumpur
Tel: 3 8660 8068
Fax: 3 8660 8070
Website: www.turkishairlines.com

Uzbekistan Airways
Tel: 3 2142 5818
Fax: 3 2145 1012

Vietnam Airlines
Tel: 3 2141 2416
Fax: 3 2142 2801
Website: www.vietnamairlines.com

Xiamen Airlines
Tel: 3 2166 8222
Fax: 3 2166 8234

Yemenia Yemen Airlines
Tel: 3 2161 6960
Fax: 3 2161 6977

appendix two

appendix two

Useful Malay words and phrases

Basics

Day	Hari
Night	Malam
Yes	Ya
No	Tidak
Rain	Hujan
Sun	Matahari
Village	Kampung
Friend	Kawan
Female	Perempuan
Male	Lelaki
Excuse me	Minta maaf
Direction	Arah
I am sorry	Saya minta maaf
Please	Tolong
Good	Elok/Bagus
Not good	Tak elok/Tak bagus
Thank you	Terima kasih
Welcome	Selamat datang
You're most welcome	Sama-sama
See you again	Jumpa lagi
Bon voyage	Selamat jalan
How much?	Berapa?
Who can I contact?	Siapa boleh saya hubung?
When?	Bila?
Destination/places	Destinasi/tempat
Sea	Laut
Beach	Pantai
Coast	Tepi laut
Island	Pulau
Mountain	Gunung
Hills	Bukit
Lakes	Tasik
Town/city	Bandar
Village	Kampung
Jungle	Hutan
Bank	Bank
Post office	Pejabat pos
Launderette	Kedai dobi
Toilet bilik air	Tandas
Public phone	Telepon awam
Bookshop	Kedai buku
Petrol station	Stesen minyak

Supermarket	Pasaraya
Market	Pasar
Night market	Pasar malam
Road	Jalan
Street	Jalan
Lane	Lorong
Dentist	Doktor gigi
Pharmacy	Famasi
Police station	Balai polis
Hospital	Hospital
Embassy	Kedutaan
Jetty	Jeti
Airport	Lapangan terbang
Bus station	Stesen bas
Taxi stand	Stesen teksi
Money changer	Penukar wang
Internet cafe	Café/kedai internet
Restaurant	Restoran
Titles	Gelaran
Miss	Cik
Mr	Encik
Mrs	Puan
Sir	Tuan
Friend	Kawan
Doctor	Doktor
Police	Polis
Uncle	Bapa saudara
Auntie	Emak saudara
Grandpa	Datuk
Grandma	Nenek
Sister (older)	Kakak
Brother (older)	Abang
Younger brother or sister	Adik
Drinks	Minuman
Black coffee (no sugar)	Kopi kosong
White coffee with less sugar	Kopi kurang manis
Black coffee with sugar	Kopi-O
Tea with milk and sugar	Teh
Milk tea, less sugar	Teh kurang manis
Tea (no sugar, no milk)	Teh kosong
Iced lemon tea	Teh-O-ice limau
Milk	susu
Sugar	gula
Ginger tea	Teh halia
Coconut milk	Air kelapa

A2

Sugar cane juice	Air tebu
Mineral water	Air mineral
Water	Air (pronounced Aa – yeh)
Hot	Panas
Cold	Sejuk
Ice	Ais
Bottled drinks	Air botol
Mineral water	Air mineral
Canned drinks	Air tin
Alcohol	Arak
Fruit juice	Jus air buah
Food	Makanan
Rice	nasi
More rice	Tambah nasi
Not too spicy	Kurang pedas
I'm vegetarian	Saya tidak makan daging
Fried noodles	Mee goreng
Fried rice	Nasi goreng
Bread	Roti
Toast	Roti bakar
Butter	Mentega
Jam	Jam
Eggs	Telur
Hard-boiled egg	Telur setengah masak
Sunny side up	Telur mata kerbau
Scrambled egg	Telur han-chur
Seafood	Makanan laut
Fish	Ikan
Squid	Sotong
Crab	Ketam
Chicken	Ayam
Beef	Daging lembu
Taste	Rasa
Spicy	Pedas
Sweet	Manis
Sour	Masam
Salty	Masin
Fried	Goreng
Steam	Rebus
Salt	Garam
Pepper	Lada hitam
I would like some …	Saya ingin nak …
I don't want any …	Saya tidak mahu …

A2

Numbers	Nombor
1	Satu
2	Dua
3	Tiga
4	Empat
5	Lima
6	Enam
7	Tujuh
8	Lapan
9	Sembilan
10	Sepuluh
11	Sebelas
12	Dua belas
20	Dua puluh
21	Dua puluh satu
30	Tiga puluh
31	Tiga puluh satu
40	Empat puluh
41	Empat puluh satu
100	Seratus
150	Seratus lima puluh
200	Dua ratus
1000	Satu ribu
10s	Puluh
Million	Juta

Days	Masa
Sunday	Ahad
Monday	Isnin
Tuesday	Selasa
Wednesday	Rabu
Thursday	Khamis
Friday	Jumaat
Saturday	Sabtu

Time	Hari
Minute	Minit
Hour	Jam
Week(s)	Minggu
Year (s)	Tahun
Tomorrow	Esok
Today	Hari ini

What time is it?	Pukul berapa?
One o'clock	Pukul satu
Half past	Setengah
Half past one	Satu setengah
Quarter past	Suku
Quarter past one	Satu suku

Colours	Warna
white	putih
black	hitam
yellow	kuning
red	merah
blue	biru
green	hijau
orange	oren
purple	ungu
pink	jambu (merah)
brown	chokolat
grey	kelabu
dark	tua (literally means old)
light	muda (*literally means young*)
light blue	biru muda
dark blue	biru tua

Greetings	Penyambutan
How are you?	Apa khabar?
Fine	Baik
Thank you	Terima kasih
Good morning	Selamat pagi
Good afternoon	Selamat tengahari
Good evening	Selamat petang
What's your name?	Apa nama awak?
My name is ...	Nama saya ialah ...

Shopping	Beli-Belah
I don't understand	Saya tidak faham
How much?	Berapa harganya?
It's too expensive	Ini telalu mahal
Can you reduce the price?	Boleh tak kurangkan harga?
Beautiful	Cantik
Do you have other colours?	Ada warna yang lain?
Any other sizes?	Ada saiz yang lain?
Do you have a larger one?	Ada yang lebih besar?
Small	Kecil
Medium	Serderhana

A2

Large	Besar
Can I change this?	Bolehkah saya tukar yang ini?

Bookings and reservations   Tempahan

How much is a standard room?	Berapa harga bilik biasa
Double bed?	Katil kembar
Single bed?	Katil seorangan?
Air conditioning/fan?	Hawa dingin/kipas?
Water heater?	Air panas?
En suite bathroom?	Bilik tidur bersama bilik mandi?
Can you confirm my reservations?	Boleh saya tetap tempahan saya?
Do you take credit cards?	Ada anda terima kad kredit?

Getting around   Jalan-jalan

I want to go ...	Saya hendak pergi ...
Where is the ...	Di mana ...
Where is the ... toilet?	Di manakah ... tandas?
Ladies	Perempuan
Men's	Lelaki
What time does it open/close?	Pukul berapa buka/tutup?
Which way is the ...	Yang mana jalan ke ...
Straight	Terus
Right	Kanan
Left	Kiri
Town	Bandar
I'm staying at ...	Saya tinggal di ...
Can you take me to ...	Boleh anda bawa saya ke ...
How do I get to.....	Bagaimana saya pergi ke ...
Are there any buses going to...	Adakah bas pergi ke ...
Where can I buy tickets ...	Di mana saya beli tiket ...
Is it free seating?	Ini tempat duduk bebaskah?
Which is the closest stop to...	Yang mana perhentian dekat ...
Arrival	Ketibaan
Departure	Perlepasan
Have I missed my bus /train/flight?	Adakah saya tertinggal bas/keretapi/pernerbangan
How far is ...	Berapa jauh ke ...
Where is the nearest station?	Di mana stesen terdekat?
Where do I catch a cab?	Dimana saya boleh ambil teksi?

A2